A GUIDE TO A
LIFE
BEYOND
IMAGINATION

Steven L. Barr

α
PRESS

A Guide To A Life Beyond Imagination

Copyright © 2019 by Steven Barr

www.CastMemberChurch.com

CAST MEMBER
CHURCH

ANAHEIM • ORLANDO • BURBANK

ISBN: 978-1-949562-99-6
LCCN: 2018962792

First Edition: 2019

Publishing: Aletheia Press

www.AletheiaPress.com

α
PRESS

Contents

Section Four: Face the Unknown

Section Five: Follow Jesus Courageously

Section Six: Light Your World Confidently

To Mom and Dad,
who have always modeled a generous faith
and encouraged me to live my life in the same way.

To Lucia,
who has put up with my God-dreams
and crazy schemes while remaining true
to her own unique call to inspire others
with the hope of Jesus.

To Marisol and Miguel,
who inspire me to be true to
what I write and true to the person
God has called me to be.

Let's Get Acquainted

Hi. I'm Steven. I've discovered most "About the Author" pages I read tend to focus on an author's accomplishments. You learn very little about who they *really are*. Throughout the course of this book, you'll learn a few things about what I do. For now, since we don't know each other, I'd like to give you an opportunity to learn a little about *who I am*.

I'M USUALLY THE LOUDEST PERSON IN THE ROOM.

This is due in part to some hearing loss I have experienced from years as a musician. But, the primary reason I raise eyebrows in a room full of people is my excitement. I get revved up about the smallest thing. It's not insincere; it's genuine and it overflows from my heart. Regardless of the conversation, no matter how mundane the subject, I discover something exciting in it. This excitement is hard for me to contain and heads often turn in my direction because of it. Is it annoying? Maybe, but I don't care. That's just how God designed me and I'm okay with it. Besides, who better to have in your corner than someone who can find reasons to get excited about something happening in your life that you can't see, point it out to you, and get you excited about it as well?

I HAVE THE GIFT OF A.D.D.

Throughout my school years, I was ridiculed by my fellow students and even teachers for my lack of attention. I was a good kid, but I couldn't stay focused for very long. Then Miss Peyton, my academics teacher in my music school, took me aside after a particularly difficult day in class. She said something that changed my life. "Steven," she began, "what you have is not a disability. It's a gift. You can see multiple things happening at the same time. You recognize patterns others don't even know exist. You can read a room full of people and know how to keep their attention."

She taught me to embrace who I was created to be and not let others try to cookie-cutter me with their personal expectations.

Miss Peyton's influence is something I offer to you. We all have some kind of issue or weakness which makes us "different." It's usually something we end up wrestling with, trying to keep it locked away so others won't criticize us or tease us. The truth is, the issue or perceived weakness is probably the exact thing God wants to draw out of you to make a difference. I'm here to inspire you to not only bring it into the open. I also want to empower you to thrive in it.

I DREAM BIG, TALK BIG, AND ACT BIG.

Maybe it's because I'm only 5'3" and a half. (That half inch matters to me.) I believe each of us—yes, I'm looking at you—can have great influence in the world. This is true no matter who we are, what we do, or where we come from. It does not matter what obstacles we face or continue to wrestle. Jesus told us we could move mountains if we had a little bit of faith. I don't apologize for wanting to be a mountain mover and neither should you.

I'm going to stretch your imagination, your ability to dream, and then show you how to act on those dreams. I don't mean vain, "I want to be famous" dreams. I'm talking about noble, "God use me to make a difference in the world, for your glory" dreams. I'm not here to be your cheerleader; I'm here to be your coach and mentor to help get you going. That being said, no one is going to be cheering louder for you than me.

I TEND TO HAVE STRONG OPINIONS.

My passion can sometimes be misinterpreted as arrogance. It is never my desire to come across that way. My perspectives are formed from experience. The church I lead is on the very edge of changing culture. I see things every day that most churches won't see for years to come. I can be passionate about helping others see what lies ahead of them. My thought process may seem beyond the comfort zones of most. I will do my very best to explain where I'm coming from. Even then, you don't have to agree with me. I'm fine with this. I've been wrong a lot. It's how I learn.

Just so you know, my theology is conservative but my methodology is fluid. I'm not afraid to challenge the status quo of a particular practice if it is going to help someone understand with greater clarity.

With my opinions comes a little sarcasm at times. I know well the look from someone who questions with their squinting eyes asking, "Are you serious or not?" But hey, Jesus had a knack for sarcasm too. Did He really want us to poke our eyes out for looking at certain things? I sure hope not. Otherwise, I couldn't be writing this and you wouldn't be reading it.

I'm going to gently challenge you to move beyond what is normal and ordinary into a life that is more adventurous and incredibly extraordinary. It's not always a comfortable transition. Sometimes I'll push a little bit to keep you moving forward. But don't worry. I'll always act out of love for you and for the purpose God has created you for.

I AM RELENTLESS.

Some might say I'm stubborn. Hopefully this isn't in a bad way. It's just I don't give up. I will adapt, evolve, change strategies, and do whatever is necessary; but I won't ever lose sight of a vision. Because of this mentality, I can be viewed as redundant, repetitive, and often repeating myself. *Do you see what I did there?*

Too often, we get distracted and off course. Long journeys can cause us to wonder if there might be a shortcut. I have spent more time *stuck* in my faith than moving forward. I've looked for every shortcut you can imagine. Spoiler alert: *There aren't any shortcuts.* Trust me, I would've found one by now.

I have learned and continue to learn how to stay unstuck, even if I'm not moving at the moment. Because of what I've learned, I can help you stay on course and remain excited about your unique God-given adventure. That's why I will remind you again and again why you are on the journey in the first place. I'll reiterate principles you have learned earlier. I'll keep you focused, much like a navigator who keeps a ship pointed in the right direction. I'll never nag you, but I'll definitely keep you on track.

WHO ARE YOU?

You will learn more about me throughout this book, but that will pale in comparison to what you will learn about yourself. What matters most to me is you see yourself how God sees you. This is much more than you could imagine. I want His vision for your life to become the rudder which steers you through the high seas of adventure you were created to sail.

Don't you think that's a quest worth pursuing?

How to Read this Book

I intentionally designed this book with 30 chapters divided into six sections. Each chapter takes about five minutes to read. I designed each chapter to be a quick read to give you time to contemplate how it speaks to you and your unique circumstances.

Because of the way this book is assembled, you are able to read it three different ways:

THE ONE DAY PLAN: Read the book in one sitting. Take the opportunity to grasp the big picture and overarching intent of the book. I recommend a nice cup of coffee or tea as accompaniment.

THE ONE WEEK PLAN: (6 days/30 minutes a day.) Read one section a day. Allow yourself room to process each section's thematic building block.

THE ONE MONTH PLAN: Read one chapter a day. Use it as a springboard for prayer and contemplation.

If you want to get the most from this book, I encourage you to do all three, in whatever order you choose. This will avail your heart and mind to truly absorb the content and empower you to put it into action.

I do not consider this book a success until you are living out its message on a daily basis.

I have hundreds of "Christian" books that I have read and then put on a shelf, rarely—if ever—to be opened again. I don't want this book to suffer a similar fate. Use it again and again. Keep it accessible. Put it somewhere you know you will see it every day.

The more familiar you become with the principles in this book, the more they will become grafted into your daily life.

My favorite books are worn, tattered, and filled with yellow highlights throughout. It is my hope this book will look the same in your possession. And more importantly, your life will become an evidence and validation of what you have read.

Introduction

I admit it. I live in a world of make believe. My sidewalks run through a Fantasyland. They also pass through a Tomorrowland, an Adventureland, and a Frontierland. And they all lead to a castle which towers high above them all.

In reality, my world is the 47 square mile property known as The Walt Disney World Resort. With four major theme parks, two water parks, 34 hotels, several golf courses, spas, and a campground—Walt Disney World is one of the most popular travel destinations in the world. It takes approximately 74,000 employees (called "Cast Members") to create the magic Disney is known for—and it has no equal.

The church I lead serves those who make this magic happen.[1]

When my family moved to Orlando to plant what is now known as "Cast Member Church," we made a commitment to be a light of hope to those who knew little or nothing about Jesus. We wanted to build a community out of those who wanted to make a difference in the world but weren't sure what that difference was or why they even had that desire.

Our family table became the hub of the church. Not a sanctuary, auditorium, or even a hotel meeting room—rather a church began around a simple dining room table. We invited Cast Members to sit, eat, talk, and share their lives with us and ours with them. Disney Cast Members from all over the world have sat in our home, sharing their fears and failures, hopes and dreams.

Our dinner table became a sacred space—and the genesis of Cast Member Church.

After hundreds of conversations and years of observation, I became increasingly aware of four types of people who consistently connected with our church:

1. **Those who had recently given their lives to Jesus and were excited about what lay ahead.**
2. **Those who were exploring Jesus and were curious to know more about Him.**
3. **Those who had followed Jesus for a long time but felt stuck in the moment.**
4. **Those who wanted to live out Jesus' Great Commission but didn't know where to start.**

It has become our norm to see all four types people in the same room, at the same time, and even in the same conversation. For a pastor, this is a dream come true!

I have come to the conclusion that all of them share one common desire: to have a life of purpose and meaning. They want to know they matter—that who they are and what they do makes a real difference in the world. Somehow, each of their paths have led them to some kind of encounter with Jesus. As I said earlier, some are excited, some are curious, some are stuck, and some just need a place to start. If we are honest, we should probably admit we see ourselves somewhere in this mix as well.

This led me to create a simple framework (more like a tool) which would help you and me to:

1.   **Discover clarity** to hear God each time He speaks.
2.   **Develop courage** to follow Jesus wherever He leads.
3.   **Demonstrate confidence** as the Holy Spirit increases our Kingdom Influence.

This book is about that tool and it will change everything in your life.

EV—ER — Y—THING!

It's called, "The Quest Compass." It's 100% biblical, Spirit-led, and will enhance your life in three incredible ways every time you use it.

1. HEAR GOD CLEARLY.

One of my first ever conversations with a Disney Cast Member was with a sweet girl who worked at Magic Kingdom. As we talked, she said the most confusing statement.

This is exactly how I heard it:

"Pot-see went one-oh-one. I was going to ask for an ER but they pulled me to pack for wishes. I passed two alphas on the way to the hub, and I had a feeling I was going to get extended."

Here's what she actually said: "**POTC** (Pirates of the Caribbean) went **101** (shut down). I was going to ask for an **ER** (Early Release) but they pulled me to **PAC** (Parade

Audience/Access Control) for **Wishes** (firework show). I passed two **Alphas** (injury/sickness requiring medical assistance) on my way to the **Hub** (the intersection point in front of Cinderella Castle which connects all lands) and I had a feeling I was going to get **extended** (asked to work past my scheduled end of shift)."

In the Cast Member culture, this lingo is called, "DisneySpeak."

I really had no idea what she had said, but I just kept smiling as if I knew what she was talking about. Right then and there, I realized if I was going to spend time with Cast Members, I would need to learn *DisneySpeak*.

You'd be surprised at the number of people I've met who think that if God speaks, He speaks in a way they wouldn't understand. With this kind of reasoning, it's not surprising that they aren't listening.

But God does speak, and He speaks your language. He knows exactly how to communicate with you so you can easily understand.

I'm not talking about English, German, Spanish or any other verbal language. I'm talking about something far more specific. He knows everything about you. After all, He's the One who designed you. He knows how to connect with you in a personal, unique, and intimate way.

Too often, we think if God is going to speak, it will come in the form of a burning bush, a thunderous voice from the sky, or handwriting on a wall. If it isn't dramatic, we assume God isn't speaking. Nothing could be further from the truth. I'm sure if God wanted to get our attention, He could do something dramatic. But more often than not, He chooses to speak in a way which is simple, clear, and understandable.

The Quest Compass is going to help you discover what it's like to hear God's voice. Maybe not audibly, but certainly in a way that you'll know it's God speaking to you.

You'll learn to separate your own thoughts from His leading. Best of all, you'll discover how easy it is to seek Him out and find He's always available and ready to talk with you.

2. FOLLOW JESUS COURAGEOUSLY.

It's one thing to hear God clearly. It's another to have the courage to do what He asks you to do, say what He asks you to say, and go where He asks you to go. It's understandable. Most people in the Bible also hesitated when God spoke to them. You're in good company.

When you follow Jesus, you can anticipate challenges. Sometimes those challenges cause you to freeze and question if He really is leading you. You feel in your heart it's the right thing to do, but for some reason—you just can't bring yourself to *do* it.

The Quest Compass will help you to identify what is working against you. It will reveal what specific hesitations you present as you wrestle with moving forward.

Once you recognize these symptomatic hesitations, you'll be able to diagnose what impedes your quest to follow Jesus. You'll learn how to push past who or what wants to keep you from fulfilling your God-given purpose.

3. LIGHT YOUR WORLD CONFIDENTLY

There's something contagious about being around someone who hears God clearly and follows Him courageously.

In darkness, we are drawn to light.
In hopelessness, we are drawn to hope.
In despair, we are drawn to joy.

Jesus said to "...let your light shine before others, that they may see your good deeds and glorify your Father in heaven."

- Matthew 5:16 NIV

This happens when you thrive in the unique adventure God has created you to live. People notice, because your life is contagious. You display what I call, "Kingdom Influence." The more they witness your thriving relationship with God, the more they desire one with Him as well. The more they see you living courageously—unencumbered by fear—the more they wonder how they could have that kind of life.

Someone who is confident in their faith and willing to lay it all on the line every single day is someone who lives an adventure. The world is looking for people like that. You can be one of those people. Truth be told, God is calling you to be one of those people.

Regardless of where you are in life, this book is about equipping you to tread new frontiers of faith.

As we prepare to move into this adventure together, allow me to speak a blessing of promise over you and where you may find yourself today:

> Blessed are you who are excited to follow Jesus
> —*for the best is yet to come.*
>
> Blessed are you who are curious about Jesus
> —*for He will make Himself known to you.*
>
> Blessed are you who feel stuck
> —*for you will soon be moving forward like never before.*
>
> Blessed are you who don't know where to start
> —*for you have already begun.*

Are you ready? Let's do this!

Steven Barr

---

1. Cast Member Church is not endorsed, supported, or acknowledged by The Walt Disney Company or any of its subsidiaries. However, Cast Member Church is specifically designed for, and dedicated to, the unique Cast Member culture.

Section One

CREATED FOR A QUEST

Now to Him who is able to do immeasurably more than all we ask or imagine, according to His power that is at work within us... - Ephesians 3:20 NIV

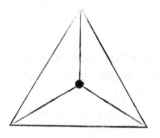

Chapter 1:
THE BEST IS YET TO COME

You could tell it would be a very warm day at Walt Disney World, but no one seemed to mind. Standing just outside Magic Kingdom, the crowd swelled in anticipation as the clock atop the train station edged closer to 9 a.m. That's when all of the waiting guests would be invited to pass through the tunnels underneath the train station to enter "the happiest place on earth."

I positioned myself on the edge of the crowd, not far from the big circular flower bed sloping down from the train station. The perfect combination of flora created the face of Mickey Mouse. I was there to meet friends. "Floral Mickey"—as it is affectionately called—was a great location to make the connection. As I waited, I passed the time by watching the crowd. Smiles abounded. Giggles and squeals came from every direction. Anticipation stirred in the air.

Close to Floral Mickey, I noticed a particular little boy. He could not have been more than four or five years old. He wore a T-shirt with Buzz Lightyear soaring across his chest. Both of his parents wore "First Visit" buttons, so I knew this was going to be a memorable and special day for all of them.

I watched this little boy, whose name happened to be Nicholas, bounce around his mom and dad like a yo-yo. He'd run a few feet from them, see something, and run back to tell them what he had seen.

"Mommy, look at the flowers!"

"Yes, Nicholas. Those are pretty."

He saw a boy with Goofy on his shirt.

"Daddy, that boy has Goofy on his shirt."

"Yes, Nicholas. That's Goofy alright."

"Daddy, will I get to see Goofy?"

"We'll do our best, Nicholas."

For the next ten minutes, Nicholas recounted to his parents every single sight, sound, and smell that surrounded him.

"Mommy, is that popcorn? Can I have some?"

"Maybe later, Nicholas. Maybe later."

Nicholas' questions were suddenly interrupted by a loud train whistle. The moment the crowd waited for was almost here. His parents pulled him close and pointed up to the train station. The courtyard erupted with music as the train steamed into the station. The crowd cheered and Nicholas' eyes and mouth widened in amazement as he recognized the passengers on the slowing train. Disney characters and princesses disembarked, smiling and waving to the cheering crowd below while singing a song of welcome. The characters had come to formally open Magic Kingdom and invite the waiting crowd into their magical domain.

Nicholas couldn't contain his excitement.

"Mommy, there's Mickey!"

"Yes, Nicholas. There's Mickey."

"Daddy, there's Donald!"

"There he is, Nicholas."

For the entire duration of the happy welcome song, Nicholas identified every character who danced and sang from the station platform. Nicholas exploded with joy. As I watched, I chuckled inwardly. I could tell his parents knew they were in for quite a day.

Finally, Mickey officially declared Magic Kingdom as open for the day and the crowds began to move forward beneath the train station and into the park. Nicholas paused and looked upward at the characters as they re-boarded the soon departing train. He sighed as he watched them pull away and out of sight.

Looking up at both of his parents he said, "That was fun! Can we go home now?"

His parents glanced at each other and smiled. They each took one of Nicholas' hands into theirs and began walking toward the entrance. As they walked away, I could hear his dad say something I will long remember:

"Oh no, the best is yet to come."

With those words, Nicholas and his parents disappeared beneath the train station into a world I knew would be tucked in his memory for the rest of his life.

I could only imagine the look on Nicholas' face as he saw Magic Kingdom for the first time. I'm sure his world was forever changed. He would never think of Disney the same way again.

Up to that moment, Nicholas had no clue what adventure lay waiting for him just beyond his expectations. Before he entered, all he knew of Magic Kingdom was a train, a few characters, and a welcome song. He had no idea the real adventure was waiting!

Nicholas was young, innocent, and certainly naive when it came to his understanding of what Walt Disney World was all about. Maybe his parents had never told him about the attractions, shows, food, or anything else on the other side of the train station. Maybe they did but his young mind simply wasn't able to form a picture of what it would be like.

For whatever reason, little Nicholas would've been content to go home having never experienced the breadth and width of Magic Kingdom. He could have left believing he saw all there was to see.

Nicholas made a permanent impression on me that day. The more I pondered that moment, the more I believe God gave me a parable for my life and yours.

As followers of Jesus, what if we are settling for less than what God offers? Jesus teaches over-and-over-and-over what the Kingdom of Heaven is like. He gives us numerous examples to describe it. But, maybe like Nicholas, we've never really understood the implications. We arrive at the gates and get excited about the characters from our favorite stories. But when the show is over and the music ends, we are ready to go home.

As followers of Jesus, what if we are settling for less than what God offers?

Christ invites us into His Kingdom. He isn't content to lead us to the entrance to observe a few stories and leave us there—outside of the adventure. There's a great quest to be discovered. We cannot experience all that has been prepared for us if we are not willing to move beyond our limited expectations and step into the adventure He offers.

However, if you are willing, I can assure you the best is yet to come!

Chapter 2:
THE PROMISE OF ADVENTURE

Millions of people visit The Walt Disney World Resort in Orlando, Florida every year. Why is it so popular? Why are families willing to save their hard-earned dollars for months, even years, to enjoy a Disney vacation? Some might say, "For escape." Maybe they're right, but I believe they are seeking something much deeper:

The promise of adventure.

Walt Disney understood the human desire to explore a world beyond the ordinary. He understood our innate hunger for adventure.

First with movies, then television, and finally theme parks—Walt quenched a deep-seated thirst to experience something beyond the borders of familiarity.

Disneyland was conceived out of his aspiration to transport guests into a completely different

31

environment. To this day, when you enter Disneyland in Anaheim, California or Magic Kingdom in Orlando, Florida, you pass beneath these words on a bronze plaque over the train station tunnels:

Here you leave today and enter the world of yesterday, tomorrow, and fantasy.

Walt Disney—unknowingly—also tapped into something God embedded into every human heart since the dawn of creation; *a desire for adventure.*

God did not create us to just survive. He created us to thrive. He gave each of us a desire to become more than who we currently are. He placed in us a longing to do something more than we are presently capable of doing.

Deep in each of our hearts we have a sense of a quest which needs to be fulfilled. And we need Him in order to explore and fulfill it.

This God-given desire for adventure is echoed in every movie, every book, and every TV show you have ever seen. I call it "The Quest." Let me show you how prevalent it is inside the stories you love.

Think of your favorite movie.

Who is the main character?

That movie encompasses a quest which includes *a call, a challenge, and a change.*

A CALL: The main character in your story is either invited into, stumbles upon, or has no choice but to answer a call to some kind of quest. They might resist the call for a while, but eventually, it must be answered.

A CHALLENGE: By answering the call, your main character crosses a threshold. They leave behind what is, and always has been, familiar to them. They now step into unfamiliar and uncharted territory. In doing so, they face a challenge.

A CHANGE: Eventually your main character confronts the challenge and discovers there is more to their identity than they previously realized. This revelation produces a change around them and within them. The situation is different from before and from this point on, the main character is different from within.

No matter the book, TV show, or movie—the quest is always the same:

A CALL. A CHALLENGE. A CHANGE.

Deep in each of our hearts we have a sense of a quest which needs to be fulfilled.

Let me give you three examples:

STAR WARS *(Lucasfilm, 1977)*

CALL: Luke Skywalker, an ordinary teenager, bored with life at home on the desert planet of Tatooine, stumbles into an opportunity to rescue a princess.

CHALLENGE: With a band of outlaws and ruffians, Luke sneaks onto the Death Star (an evil weapon of ultimate power in the galaxy) and encounters obstacle after obstacle to reach the princess.

CHANGE: With the princess rescued, Luke is now given the opportunity to destroy the Death Star through a power within him he never knew existed until the climactic moment.

BEAUTY AND THE BEAST
(Walt Disney Feature Animation, 1991)

CALL: Belle's eccentric father is held captive by a beast in a castle and Belle must rescue him.

CHALLENGE: Out of love for her father, Belle trades her father's freedom for hers instead. Now, she must figure out how to escape. She soon discovers there is more to the Beast than she previously realized.

CHANGE: Belle ends up falling in love with the Beast and saves his life. She breaks the curse which made him what he was.

POLLYANNA *(Walt Disney Productions, 1960)*

CALL: Upon the death of her missionary parents, a young girl named Pollyanna is sent to a small town in America. She lives with her aunt, the domineering town matriarch who controls everyone, including the local church.

CHALLENGE: Pollyanna soon discovers a dark cloud of negativity hangs over the town because of her aunt's firm, controlling grip. This young girl sets out to inspire citizens of the town to see how life can be so much better by simply letting go of their pessimism.

CHANGE: Pollyanna's influence inspires the town to pushback against her aunt's control. They rediscover the simple joy which had been missing from their daily lives. In a sudden plot-twist toward the end of the story, Pollyanna's own positivity is tested when tragedy strikes and the town has the opportunity to be a light in her life.

Every quest includes some kind of call, challenge, and resulting change. You do not have a story without all three. If any element is missing, the story is incomplete and not worth telling. Let me show you what I mean:

Here are two plot lines to compare:

1. *A girl finds a treasure map inside a hollow tree but tears it up into small pieces and throws it away. She never gives it another thought for the rest of her life.*

It's not much of a story, is it?

2.   *A girl finds a treasure map inside a hollow tree, tears the map into small pieces and throws the map away. The next day she finds the map completely whole, inside the same tree. Out of curiosity, she decides to learn what the map is all about and follows where it leads.*

Now there's a story!

The difference between a bad story and a good story is how the main character responds to the call. If the main character doesn't answer the call, there is no quest. But if the main character willingly (or even reluctantly) responds to the call, you have a story worth following.

God has hard-wired you and me for a quest. It's why we love a good story. These tales reflect our hibernating hopes and dreams. Adventures resonate with our aspirations. We love the idea of answering a call and rising to the challenge to cause a change. It's in our DNA.

You can choose to live vicariously through the quests created by Hollywood *or* you can actually embrace your own God-given adventure. I encourage you to step into the quest you are uniquely created to follow.

This is your invitation to a life beyond imagination.

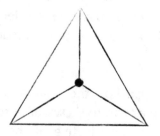

Chapter 3:
TRUE LIFE ADVENTURES

I am not a fan of Bible stories or Bible characters.

Well, let me clarify: I am not a fan of the *terms* Bible "stories" or Bible "characters."

When we refer to events in the Bible as "stories," we place them on the same mental shelf which catalogues legends and fairytales. They're interesting to read and even inspiring, yet a chasm can exist between what we read and what we *really* believe.

"The Little Mermaid" is a story. Moses parting the Red Sea, on the other hand, is a true-life adventure. You might be thinking, "Well, duh! The difference is obvious."

I don't think the difference is as obvious as we assume. The same applies when we use the term Bible "character." When historical individuals recorded in a Biblical narrative are referred to as "characters," we unintentionally slip them into the same category with people like Indiana Jones and Captain Jack Sparrow.

In case you didn't know, neither one of those people really existed. But in the Bible, when you read about a young shepherd named David, who killed a giant, you're reading a historical account of a person who actually existed.

Maybe it's cynicism or the realization of our own limitations, but we tend to skew our perceptions of God based on our own perspective of the Bible. We may struggle to believe God could work in and through us in the way He did with individuals found on the pages of Scripture because we think they were more than we ever could be.

This skewed perspective doesn't happen overnight. The transition is subtle. Here's how I believe it starts: If you grew up in the church you probably remember being in Sunday School, Kid's Church, Jr. Church, JAM! (Jesus and Me), or some other ministry for kids and youth. In those spaces, we learned Bible "stories." We were taught about the lives of Bible "characters." These characters were—albeit unintentionally—elevated to "superstar status" because of their accomplishments. We began to believe they were somehow better than us. Their stories were told in the same way legends are passed down from generation-to-generation.

Noah built the ark.
Abraham prepared to sacrifice his son, Isaac.
Moses faced down Pharaoh.
Joshua fought the battle of Jericho.
David stood before Goliath.

The list could go on-and-on.

The surprising truth is there was nothing better or "super" about any of them.

If we went back in time to ask them what it was like to be a hero of the faith—they would laugh and explain how they were the complete opposite. They would simply describe themselves as having been ordinary people with jaw-dropping flaws who faced overwhelming obstacles and desperately clung to God in whom they placed their trust.

Yet, that's not how we tend to see them.

Somewhere along the line, these individuals were elevated above our normal, everyday lives. We convinced ourselves we could admire these Bible characters from afar but never up close and personal—as models to follow.

They became engrained in our minds as separate from the realities of our human existence.

The reality of the events and people found throughout the Bible come down to this: God calls ordinary people into extraordinary challenges so they can change their world and reveal His glory.

Every name and narrative documented in Scripture follows the same pattern of a CALL, a CHALLENGE, and a CHANGE.

NOAH

GOD'S SALVATION AND A NEW BEGINNING

BUILD AN ARK TO SAVE CREATION

CHANGE

CALL

CHALLENGE

120 YEARS OF CONSTRUCTION, RIDICULE, PERSEVERANCE

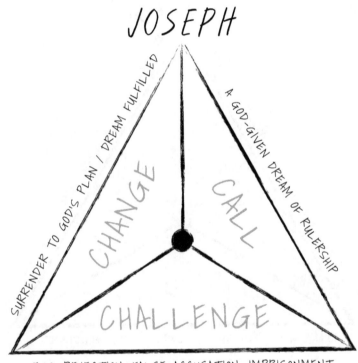

MOSES

SEES THE PROMISED LAND WITH HIS OWN EYES

FREE GOD'S PEOPLE / LEAD THEM TO PROMISED LAND

CHANGE

CALL

CHALLENGE

PHARAOH, ISRAELITES, 40 YEARS IN THE WILDERNESS

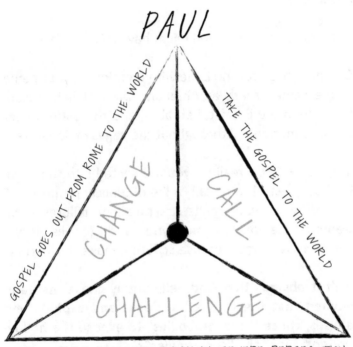

PAUL

GOSPEL GOES OUT FROM ROME TO THE WORLD

TAKE THE GOSPEL TO THE WORLD

CHANGE

CALL

CHALLENGE

SINFUL PAST, REJECTED BY MANY, SEVERE PERSECUTION

Noah, Joseph, Moses, Ruth, Esther, Peter, and Paul are all people we admire. We see them as men and women whom God used to demonstrate His love, truth, mercy, and grace. Of course, you can add hundreds of other names mentioned throughout the biblical narrative. Each one adds another branch in the great adventure.

But there's one name you might have missed: *Yours*.

God has absolutely no issue with mentioning your name in the same breath as Abraham, David, Elijah, Isaiah, Mary, John the Baptist, Barnabas, and the entire roster of those mentioned throughout the pages of Scripture.

In reality—God's reality—you are invited into the same kind of quest I like to call "a life of Biblical proportion." Regardless of your faults, fractures, or failures—God wants to use you to change your world for His glory. I know this for a fact because Scripture makes it clear:

Isn't it obvious that God deliberately chose men and women that the culture overlooks and exploits and abuses, chose these "nobodies" to expose the hollow pretensions of the "somebodies"?

- Corinthians 1:27 MSG

This includes you. It may seem hard to believe, but He lists you in the same category with the other ordinary people He chose to work through to do extraordinary things.

Every one of them answered a call, faced a challenge, and provoked a change. But unlike stories from books, movies, and TV shows— these were true-life adventures.

Regardless of your faults, fractures, or failures— God wants to use you to change your world for His glory.
BIG IDEA

You are not a character in a story. You are a real person embarking upon a real quest God has set before you. He has designed you for this quest and no other person on this planet—past, present, or future—can be who you were created to be or do what you were created to do.

As you embark upon this journey, you may not be able to hear it but there are millions-and-millions of those who have adventured before you shouting joyfully and passionately down from Heaven over-and-over again....

"C'mon!"

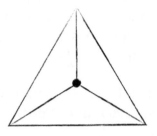

Chapter 4:
Listen, Leap, and Learn

Years ago, I taught worship theology at a worship leader college in Durango, Mexico. Young people from all over the Spanish-speaking world came to develop their music and leadership gifts. These were some of the brightest, most talented, and most spiritually savvy young people I ever met. Their passion for Jesus was inspiring. I probably learned more from them than they ever learned from me.

One day, a student from Argentina invited me to come play fútbol (or soccer, as my U.S. friends call it) with a group of students on the upcoming Saturday morning. I was excited they wanted to include me. I said "yes" without hesitation.

After telling my wife, Lucia, about accepting the invitation, she simply responded by rolling her eyes and offering a sarcastic, *"Ooooookay."*

My wife is from Mexico and has fútbol in her blood. She knew a short guy from Columbus, Ohio might not fare so well on the field with a bunch of people who eat, live, and breathe soccer. I assured her they would respect me as their teacher. Surely they would have Christ-like compassion on someone who was not as competent in the sport.

Even as I walked out the door on Saturday morning, Lucia asked, "Are you sure you want to do this?"

"Oh sweetie, I'll be just fine," I replied reassuringly.

I was *so* wrong.

Fast forward 90 minutes. Lucia heard a scratching-like sound at the front door. She opened it cautiously.

There standing before her were the remnants of what used to be her husband. I was covered head-to-toe with dirt. My shirt was torn. I was bleeding in several places. (Minorly of course, but hey—blood drawn is blood drawn.) My legs were bruised. I couldn't lift my arms. The scratching Lucia heard at the door was me as I tried to get my key in the lock but I was not able to focus. I'm sure I looked like someone who was inebriated after a long night at the local cantina.

But none of this had happened. It was just me, looking like I had returned from battle. Lucia actually wondered, for a split-second, if I had been mugged. After looking me up and down for several seconds, my always compassionate, mercy-filled wife paused for a moment— then broke out laughing uncontrollably.

Not exactly the sympathetic reaction I desired.

She walked me into the house and very slowly took me upstairs to our room. I couldn't move any part of my body without feeling sharp pain. By the way, she never stopped laughing the entire time. She's a real sweetheart.

Over the next few days, I discovered muscles in my body I never knew I had. I discovered them because for the first time ever—they hurt. Soccer is one of those sports in which every muscle in your body is utilized to some capacity. If you don't normally use them, you'll never know they exist until you play soccer.

Looking back, I realized I never prepared to play a soccer match at the same level as my students. They had played the game their entire lives. They knew how to fall, how to absorb the hits, and how to avoid being tripped. I didn't because I wasn't prepared. I limped home— vowing to never play the game again. It wasn't worth it.

Following God can feel a lot like how I felt that gray, Saturday morning.

We can get bloodied and bruised easily if we are not prepared. We mentally and emotionally love the idea of a God-given adventure we are created for. But if we haven't trained for it, we may walk off the field feeling beaten.

Perhaps at some point in your walk with God, you took a faith-action. You felt sure He had led you in a particular direction. But you got pummeled. You felt foolish and ended up limping away. Perhaps you vowed to never do something "stupid" like that again. I know this feeling all too well.

But here's what I've learned: Following Jesus takes practice, discipline, getting knocked down, and getting back up. When we first start, we are going to get it wrong a lot. But we can't let those setbacks discourage us. No one gets it right from the start. Have you ever mastered something at the very beginning?

Does someone pick up a guitar for the very first time and sound like a virtuoso?

Does someone hit a golf ball perfectly the first time he or she swings a club?

Does a recipe turn out exactly the way a novice chef wants the first time they make it?

Of course not. It takes practice, patience, and perseverance. When we follow Jesus, there are three areas of life we absolutely must exercise with the greatest discipline:

LISTEN: We tune our spiritual ears to recognize when God is speaking to us.

LEAP: We move forward in faith, trusting that God is with us no matter what.

LEARN: We observe what God reveals as a result of our obedience.

BIG IDEA

Following Jesus takes practice, discipline, getting knocked down, and getting back up.

Let's look at them on the triangle of CALL, CHALLENGE, and CHANGE:

Imagine you could hear God clearly in the midst of a noisy world that screams for your attention. (**LISTEN**)

You can if you develop your ability to listen.

Imagine you could follow Jesus courageously regardless of whatever may stand in your way. (**LEAP**)

You can if you develop your ability to leap,
no matter what.

Imagine you could be a light in the darkness, confidently shining no matter the context. (**LEARN**)

You can if you develop your ability to learn
and adapt as God leads.

As a follower of Jesus, isn't that what you want? The whole point of this book is to prepare you for the adventure waiting for you. Yes, there will be times when it's going to hurt. There will be moments when you want to give up. You might even catch yourself wondering if it is actually worth it.

That's normal and you are far from being alone in thinking it.

But by the time we finish this journey together, you'll have begun to experience the clarity, courage, and confidence to live the quest God has uniquely designed you for.

That's a promise.

Section Two

THE DNA OF YOUR QUEST

"Before I formed you in the womb I knew you, before you were born I set you apart; I appointed you as a prophet to the nations." - Jeremiah 1:5 NIV

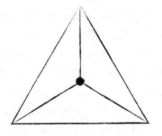

CHAPTER 5:
MICKEY MOUSE EXPLAINS
THE MEANING OF LIFE

We each have specific days which are etched in our memory—moments we'll never forget. Maybe for you it was the day of your graduation, your wedding, the birth of your children, or the passing of someone close to you. Moments like these never fade. They are as real today as the day they happened.

For me, one particular moment changed my life forever. You'll think I'm exaggerating when I tell you what occurred, but I swear every word is true. It really happened and since that day I've never been the same.

I want to tell you about the day Mickey Mouse explained the meaning of life to me.

Many autumns ago, I walked down Main Street U.S.A. at Magic Kingdom. As I slowly strolled from beneath the shadows of the train station into the bright Florida sunshine, the smell of freshly-popped popcorn grabbed my attention.

It was around 10 a.m. and too early for popcorn, so I willed myself away from the nearby cart. I maneuvered through the crowds into the town square. The air filled with the four-part harmonies of a live barbershop quartet who entertained the crowd gathering around them. Enhancing the music were the squeals of children, who led (more like dragged) their moms and dads by the hand toward the centerpiece of Magic Kingdom: Cinderella Castle. The crowd flittered toward the castle like fallen leaves being gently carried on a breeze down a neighborhood street.

I took my time as I meandered along the sidewalk, casually looking in the windows of the specialty stores along Main Street. Kids and adults emerged from the Chapeau Hat Shop with traditional Mickey ears— freshly embroidered with their names. The Confectionary sold sweets of every size, shape, and savor. I peered into a window where a Disney Cast Member decorated freshly chocolate-dipped strawberries on the other side of the glass. She smiled and waved as she placed a tray of those beauties right in front of me.

Next came Main Street Cinema, which wasn't a movie theatre anymore. The whimsical storefront offered an array of Disney artwork. As I passed underneath the marquee, I glanced toward the window. In an instant, my casual stroll came to a screeching halt. I don't know if I can adequately capture with words how I felt the moment I saw it.

All I know is it took my breath away. I couldn't stop staring at it. There was something about it which wouldn't let me go.

It was a painting, a painting of Mickey Mouse.

In my lifetime, especially during my recent years as pastor of Cast Member Church, I've seen hundreds—even thousands—of paintings, drawings, and sculptures of Mickey Mouse. But something deep and meaningful made this painting different. To this day, I have never felt so moved by a picture of Mickey or any picture for that matter.

In this particular painting, Mickey sat on a stool. He had a big canvas placed upon an art easel in front of him and a paintbrush in his hand. Mickey stared into a mirror—studying his own features the way an artist would when attempting to capture and create a self-portrait. Only this was not a self-portrait. What Mickey saw in the mirror and what came from Mickey's brush were two different things.

The image on the canvas was not the likeness of Mickey Mouse, but rather the face of Walt Disney—Mickey's creator.

When Mickey Mouse peered into the mirror, he beheld the face of his creator.

Time stood still as I stared at the painting. People passed behind me and in front of me, totally oblivious to the masterpiece in their midst. I couldn't believe how people didn't notice what I saw in this beautiful work of art. Something amazing happened to me there in front of the painting; God spoke these words into my heart:

"This is the meaning of life."

According to who I know for certain was God, this painting revealed an answer to a question I didn't know I had been asking.

I finally tore myself away from the painting. I joined my friends for a day filled with riding attractions and seeing shows throughout Magic Kingdom. Regardless of what we did, that painting continued to linger in my mind.

After the nighttime fireworks, we walked back down Main Street toward the exit. I went to see the painting one more time. While I took what I thought was my final look, a Cast Member at the entrance near the window informed me I could purchase a print of that very painting. I didn't even ask her how much it was. I left Magic Kingdom that night with my message from God, rolled up and sealed in a round canister.

Within a week, I had it framed. To this day, it has hung in either my home or my office— front and center for all to see. If you want to take a look, you can see it on my office wall in the photo on the back cover of this book.

To me, that painting has become a foundational visual of the quest we all long to pursue. Deep inside, we intrinsically know we are created to reflect more than just ourselves to the world. What Mickey so eloquently revealed in that painting was how *our* purpose is to reflect the very essence of our Creator.

Many years have passed. I now live less than a mile from the location where I first saw the original. I treasure the significance of this painting more with each passing day.

What could be so powerful about a painting—especially one of Mickey Mouse—to cause a person to discover with indescribable clarity, the meaning of life? The answer is found in the mirror; the mirror Mickey Mouse looked into.

You are a reflection of the One who created you.

When I walked down Main Street U.S.A. and happened to glance into a window at a painting of Mickey Mouse, God changed my life in an instant. He gave me a picture to remind me that to see His reflection in the mirror is my deepest longing. It is what gives my life meaning.

Even now, as I write these words in my office, that painting looks over my shoulder. I wish you could see Mickey's face. It's as if he's encouraging each of us to look in the mirror and get ready to see something we've never seen before.

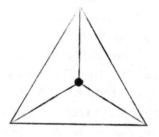

CHAPTER 6:
THE BREATH OF LIFE

If you talk to either one of my kids for more than sixty seconds you will discover both Marisol and Miguel are reflections of my wife and I. Marisol looks more like her mom but has my artistic personality and temperament. She'll deny it, but it's true. Miguel looks just like me except he has Lucia's thick hair. He also inherited his mother's laid back attitude and is incredibly mellow. Marisol and Miguel are reflections of their parents—yet they are incredibly unique people. They may carry a little of my DNA and a little of Lucia's DNA, but both of them are *one-and-onlys*.

Thanks to science, and sources such as Ancestry.com, we know every person is a "one-and-only" because of their unique DNA. That tiny, microscopic double-helix which determines hair shade, eye color, bone structure, skin tone, and a thousand other attributes is responsible for defining each and every one of us. It's our DNA which makes us unique. Yet, even "identical" twins are not truly identical.

Lucia and I are friends with three sisters from New Zealand who are identical triplets. In fact, they are the only identical triplets to have ever worked at Walt Disney World together. When I first met Kailee, Alesha, and Chantelle—I honestly could not tell them apart. I was afraid to call any one of them by name for fear I would address the wrong one. A few weeks ago, we all sat at the dining room table in our home. I began to notice subtle but wonderful differences between the three of them. They may have appeared identical to me when I first met them, but now I was able to see them for who they really were—three wonderfully unique young ladies. No matter what we have in common or how similar we may appear, each of us is exquisitely unique.

Of course, we don't have to look under a microscope to see what makes us different. Have you ever met someone who was a photocopy of yourself? I didn't think so. You are *you* because of your DNA.

You also have another form of DNA. This DNA has nothing to do with your eyes, hair, height, or anything else regarding the way you look. This double helix is your *spiritual* DNA. Even before you were conceived, God designed you to reflect the essence of who He is in a way that no other person in this world— past, present, or future—could. Just like your physical DNA, your spiritual DNA is one-of-a-kind, but infinitely more significant than your physical body.

It's the *soul* of who you are.

 BIG IDEA Just like your physical DNA, your spiritual DNA is one-of-a-kind, but infinitely more significant than your physical body.

To understand this, we have to go to the first chapter of Genesis. Let's look at the place in the Bible which introduces us to God as He creates the universe.

He creates light and sky.
He forges land and oceans.
He creates plants, fruits, and vegetables.
He fashions stars, planets, and moons.
He forms birds and fish.
He creates animals which walk and crawl on the ground.

Each time He *speaks* a new aspect of creation into being, *BOOM!* It comes into existence. It is here where the narrative shifts as God prepares for the climax of His creation:

God spoke: "Let us make human beings in our image, make them reflecting our nature so they can be responsible for the fish in the sea, the birds in the air, the cattle, and, yes, Earth itself, and every animal that moves on the face of Earth."

God created human beings; He created them godlike, reflecting God's nature. He created them male and female.

God blessed them: "Prosper! Reproduce! Fill Earth! Take charge! Be responsible for fish in the sea and birds in the air, for every living thing that moves on the face of Earth."

-Genesis 1:26-28 MSG

Twice in just three verses God refers to humanity as reflections of His nature. He never bestows such honor upon any other part of creation. A little further into the narrative, we read the details of how God actually created human beings:

God formed man out of dirt from the ground and blew into his nostrils the breath of life. The man came alive—a living soul!

- Genesis 2:7 MSG

As God created humanity, He did something with the man He never did with any other element of creation: God breathed into His nostrils the *breath of life*.

There was something incredibly different about this breath of life.

Lots of animals within God's creation breathe. Horses breathe. Dogs breathe. Dolphins breathe. Sheep breathe. Even the chameleon sitting outside my office window as I type this is breathing. But nowhere in the Bible is it recorded an animal received "the breath of life" from God. He didn't breathe into animals like He did with Adam. *But, why did God do this for Adam?*

God set him apart to be *spiritually alive*. When God breathed into Adam, He gave him a gift which was unique amidst all of creation.

He gave Adam a soul. The first human was exclusively designed to reflect the glory of His Creator. For this reflection to happen, he needed a soul. This soul gave Adam the capacity to love, create, and imagine—just like his Creator.

As Adam's offspring, you too have a soul, filled with the same breath of life. You are a reflection of God; a living mirror capable of revealing a glimpse of your Creator to anyone who sees you. It's the reason you exist.

The more you become aware of how you are designed to reflect Him and follow His ways—thus becoming like Him—the more others will see Him on display. Such influence has the potential to ignite their desire to reflect Him as well.

The entire purpose of your quest is for God's reflection to become as brilliant and life-giving to others as possible. The closer you move toward Him—the brighter His reflection becomes.

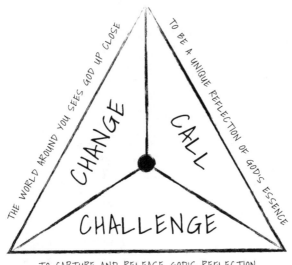

TO CAPTURE AND RELEASE GOD'S REFLECTION

That breath from God which gave life to your soul contains a unique and purposed *call to change* the world around you. But remember: it's just a reflection.

Learning how to capture and release this reflection is the *challenge*. Once you understand and begin to do it, everything *changes*.

Your reflection is no longer about you; it's about God shining brilliantly in you and from you.

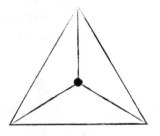

CHAPTER 7:
WHO AM I
AND WHY AM I HERE?

When I was a child, I remember playing with a mirror in the sun. I would fix the mirror on the sun, angle it just right, and then re-aim it elsewhere. I often aimed it at someone else. It was all about capturing the light just right and releasing it to where I wanted it to go, thus catching the attention of anyone I chose.

It's the same with God's reflection. The light is captured; then the light is released. This means there are two dynamics necessary for us to reflect God's nature. The more we thrive in each of these areas determines how brightly His nature is revealed.

God's life-giving breath which filled Adam's soul initiated these two dynamics which are not found in any other being in creation:

A RELATIONSHIP with God and a RESPONSIBILITY on behalf of God.

God gave Adam and Eve an identity found only in a *relationship* with Him. He also gave them a *calling* fulfilled only through a *responsibility* on His behalf. Both of these are at the heart of your quest.

Adam and Eve enjoyed a perfect relationship with God as they walked with Him and conversed with Him—much like children walking with their father. No secrets. No fears. They were absolutely safe and secure in their identity as God's kids. It was a perfect union.

Adam and Eve also carried out a perfect responsibility on His behalf. They represented Him as caretakers of the world He created. They were in charge. They embraced their calling by exercising their God-given authority over the earth while also submitting with complete trust to God's authority over their lives.

But since Adam and Eve chose to exercise their free-will in opposition to God's order—things went terribly wrong. Before we go there, let's linger awhile in the Garden of Eden before Satan made his first appearance in the human drama and caused it to all fall apart.

As we attempt to grasp the perfect order God placed in the lives of Adam and Eve, when the world was new—we have an opportunity to understand why *we* were created. Let's look at your relationship with God through the lens of the quest and see the simple, yet profound beauty of God's design.

RELATIONSHIP QUEST

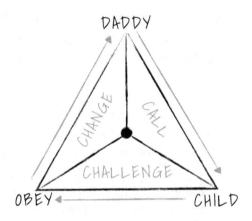

God designed Adam and Eve to enjoy a deep, meaningful relationship with Him. Because of that breath of life; having a soul gave them an identity with God. They wouldn't be God, but they would be a part of Him much like children to their daddy. My children are not identical copies of me, yet they definitely have a lot of me in them.

You may wonder why I choose the word, "Daddy" to describe God. There is nothing wrong with addressing Him with the more formal approach of "Father." But I use "Daddy" because He is so much more than just a father. Jesus called Him, "Abba"—which in Hebrew equates to "Daddy."

The Message version of the Bible presents us with a beautiful slant on the word.

This resurrection life you received from God is not a timid, grave-tending life. It's adventurously expectant, greeting God with a childlike, "What's next, Papa (Daddy)?"

- Romans 8:15 MSG

When Marisol was a little girl, she always called me "Papa." It always filled my heart with joy. I'm sure it does the same thing for God's heart when we talk with Him in the same manner.

As "Daddy" to Adam and Eve, God provided for their every need. He modeled what it meant to love so they, in turn, could know how to love their own children. Between their creation and their fall, we know Adam and Eve loved God and trusted all He said and did. They had no reason to doubt because they knew they were wholly loved and complete. This secure foundation as His children gave them a confident standing to obey whatever He asked of them. They knew He always had their welfare in mind.

At this point of the narrative, it was never really a challenge for Adam and Eve to trust God without condition. Since temptation was yet to be an issue, trust was a choice they could easily make.

Their simple obedience was confirmation of their trust in their Daddy. They knew He was true to His word and could be completely depended upon. There was no reason for them to think otherwise.

We are designed no different from Adam and Eve. But, trust is far more of a challenge for us because of reasons I will explore shortly. For now, let's stay focused on how things were supposed to be.

God is your Daddy. He lovingly guides you, nurtures you, and protects you. As His child, you are called to trust Him no matter what; He always knows what's best for you.

This trust leads to unconditional obedience; even when you are challenged with an incomplete picture of what will come next.

When you obey, you reflect God's righteousness, revealing His nature to those around you.

A mirror can only reflect what it's fixed upon. Since you are created for a relationship with God, you must remain focused on Him. If not, His reflection from you will dim and others are not going to see Him. This is why your relationship with God must always be attended to and never left in neglect. Otherwise, you will begin reflecting something other than God. That never ends well.

Adam and Eve weren't only created for a relationship. They were also created for a responsibility: to rule over the earth. God was not only their Daddy; He was also their King. As their King, He gave them the authority to represent Him to all of creation. After all, they were His kids. They were caretakers of all He made. With that authority came a mission:

"Prosper. Reproduce. Fill the Earth. Take charge!"

Just as we inherit the same standing of relationship with God that Adam was designed for, we also have inherited the responsibility piece.

Here's what responsibility looks like through the lens of the quest:

RESPONSIBILITY QUEST

God is your King; He calls you to commit yourself in His service. As His child, you have His authority. You are called to speak and act on His behalf. With that authority, you embrace the challenge of a mission—to make Him known. In the fulfillment of that mission, He changes the world through you.

The relationship with your Daddy and responsibility to your King will shape an overarching, lifetime quest. This quest is built upon thousands of daily quests, each one reinforcing trust, authority, obedience, and mission.

As you move further into your quest, the world will recognize God in you—before they even recognize you.

That's a pretty amazing thought. Here's why I believe it will happen: God's design for relationship and responsibility are the answers to the two most often asked philosophical questions from our world today:

WHO AM I?

I am a child of the one true God...
(*RELATIONSHIP/IDENTITY*)

WHY AM I HERE?

...endowed with authority to represent Him to the world.
(R*ESPONSIBILITY/CALLING*)

If you and I truly understood the answers to both of those questions, imagine what our lives could be like and what possibilities would lie ahead.

Adam and Eve certainly understood the answers. But so did Satan. The Thief and Father of Lies knew something had to be done to destroy these God-reflections before they had a chance to multiply and fill the earth.

Satan knew that when God created Adam and Eve, He gave each of them the freedom of choice. He didn't create them as mindless robots who had no choice but to obey every word He spoke. He made them with living souls with the ability to love. As we know—love must be a choice. Within the framework and order of creation— God warned them that choosing to disobey would invite unimaginably painful consequences.

The consequence of disobedience meant they would die and be separated from God's provision and protection. Their reflection of His glory and nature would be extinguished.

Enter the serpent.

Why be a reflection of God when you could shine on your own? After all, wouldn't you want to be like God?

This sums up the temptation Satan offered them.

Maybe they hadn't thought about it before? Maybe up to that moment they had been completely content to be mirrors of God's nature? Satan must have made the proposal quite attractive for them to consider such a dangerous offer. The thought of making themselves the point of the mirror's focus was just too tempting. Perhaps Satan created a sliver of doubt which caused them to wonder if God was holding out on them? For just a moment—they set aside their security as His children. They disassociated themselves from God's good, loving nature and lost sight of His protection and provision for all they ever needed.

Adam and Eve sided with the serpent's suggestion. They rebelled against God's design. They exercised their free-will *against* God. In turn, with their disobedience enacted, they looked at themselves in the mirror expecting to see the same glory and nature that had been there before—but it wasn't. There was no glory. There was no God-nature. There was no security, provision, or protection. All they saw were themselves completely exposed. Naked. Vulnerable. In horror, they knew they had been lied to by the serpent.

From the moment Adam and Eve rebelled against God's perfect and loving plan for their lives, everything came crashing down. The mirror of God's nature that He had created for them shattered into thousands of irreparable pieces. They could no longer be with God in His presence. Sin prevented them from being His reflection. The world went spiritually dark. Creation was introduced to the malignant cancer of sin.

Satan's deception injected a distrust of God's nature into humanity. This led to a rebellious nature which has been inherited by each generation after. Every man, woman, and child since has sought to pick up the pieces of their mirrors only to realize the brokenness is irreparable. No human hand could ever restore the reflection of God.

All had been lost—or so it seemed.

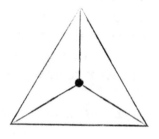

CHAPTER 8:
SHATTERED

Hopelessness is the most horrible feeling a person can experience. There's no way up or down; no way in or out. Like a cold-blooded snake, it paralyzes and suffocates its victims with merciless indifference.

If you've ever sat in a doctor's office and heard the words, "I'm sorry. There's nothing more we can do," you've felt the squeezing of hopelessness. You've known what it's like to see your world come crashing down in an instant. Your body goes numb. Your mind is unable to process. Everything seems to move in slow motion as your world falls to pieces.

This was the excruciating reality for Adam and Eve. They made a choice and paid with their souls. Their disobedience has impacted the life of every human being after them. They were deceived into believing their own reflection would be as glorious as God's reflection. What they didn't realize was without God's glory—they had no glory of their own.

Adam and Eve were once beautiful reflections of God, in perfect relationship with God, and perfect representatives of God. But this was shattered into thousands of tiny shards. The aftermath only allowed them to pick up one piece at a time to see a small glimpse of what once was and what could've been.

In the end, all they had was hopelessness.

To this day, humanity searches desperately through the pile of broken shards hoping to find that God-reflection. We may catch a quick sparkle of identity here and a shimmer of calling there. We crave true relationship. But outside of God, we only find fleeting slivers of what a meaningful bond looks like. For the vast majority of the world, these specks may seem enough. Yet deep down, a hunger remains. Slowly, we come to the realization that these passing moments don't come close to the relational fulfillment we all ache for.

The same discontent happens in the realm of responsibility. Every person in the world wants to accomplish something—to make a dent of meaningful impact in the universe. We want to know what we do matters. The result? Humanity digs through the shattered pieces of their God-reflection—picking up fragments and splinters of what true calling looked like. Again, we often settle for what we can hold in our fingers. We seek meaning and purpose from countless sources. We build a world around our jobs, talents, and accomplishments. But it is to no avail. Humanity still feels the empty hopelessness Adam and Eve introduced into our world, as the serpent mocks us from the shadows.

But God did not give up on Adam and Eve, nor does He give up on humanity. Abandoning His purpose for us is not in His nature. Though we failed Him—He never fails us. Though we walked away from our identity as His children—He still holds to His identity as our perfectly loving Daddy. Part of that divine nature means He still has a plan to provide and protect us.

God, the Daddy/King created Adam and Eve and called them to bear His name—to carry His authority throughout the earth. In their disobedience, their mission was derailed. But the omnipotent, omnipresent, and omniscient God of all that is seen and unseen could never be deterred. His purposes for humanity would move forward. They would once again become His reflection through His plan for restoration.

How He would accomplish it would be indescribably amazing.

It is imperative to understand that God *IS* holiness, love, truth, mercy, and grace. These are not separate categories. They are one and they are God. He doesn't compromise truth for love. His truth *IS* love and His love *IS* truth. He doesn't sacrifice holiness for mercy. His holiness is mercy and His mercy is holy. This matters because God's plan required Him to stay within the order He created. He would not bend the rules for Adam and Eve—nor does He do that for us. He meant it when He said Adam and Eve would die for their disobedience. But what if God's plan involved a way in which the dead came back to life? What if their lifeless souls could be redeemed—vibrantly alive with His reflection once more?

God had a plan to restore humanity to its reflective purpose even before He created the world. Think about *THAT* for a second. God created Adam and Eve knowing all along they would rebel against Him and exchange His nature for a sinful nature. The purpose God designed for humanity would move forward no matter what. He already had a plan in place.

Isn't that amazing?

BIG IDEA God had a plan to restore humanity to its reflective purpose even before He created the world.

Throughout the Old Testament, humanity searched for the divine reflection they longed for and yet they rejected God at every turn. Though God repeatedly extended His hand to direct them towards Himself, He made one thing clear. If men and women were to reflect Him once again it would be on His terms, not theirs. For the most part, humanity was content to continue searching through broken shards for a glimmer of hope. They turned to every broken source except the only One who could actually restore them. Coming to God on His terms meant they would need to admit they were wrong. It also required them to turn their backs from the broken sources they created for themselves. In essence, to regain their God-given quests, they would have to give up on their own self-made quests.

To be God's reflection once again, they had to reject their sinful nature. Yet even when a few tried, they quickly discovered they could never live up to God's expectations. In turn, they figured, "Why bother?" God's holiness demanded perfection. Because they no longer bore His reflection; they could never be perfect. It was an impossible cycle. It simply couldn't be done.

Hopelessness ensued.

Yet, God knew all along that it couldn't be done alone. He allowed humanity to recognize it needed Him to fulfill their created identity and calling. You and I can never be whole apart from God. We can't be good enough. No matter how hard we try, the perfection He requires will never be achieved by our own human efforts.

But all of these factors in play cause us to ask the question, "Why would God set a standard so high that no man or woman could ever reach it?" To some, this may seem like God is cruel. I've had countless conversations with people who perceive God as unfair because He "demands" perfection from people. It's true He is holy (righteous, perfect) and He requires nothing less than that standard from us. Before they rebelled, this was the standard Adam and Eve had within their perfect relationship with God. Of course, this was before they chose to reject Him.

Since the tragedy in the Garden of Eden, humanity has done everything in its power to return to paradise—to recapture that God-reflection. Even in our best expressions of love, truth, mercy, and grace—we fall massively short of holiness. The reflection we long for remains a pile of jagged shards. Of our own ability, we could never restore the shattered mirror.

But God was about to step in. From before the Garden rebellion, He had a plan. At the moment they sinned, it sprang into motion. He would raise up hope out of the heap of hopelessness. He would put the pieces together once again.

But first, He would have to shatter another mirror.

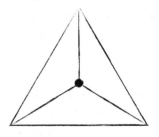

CHAPTER 9:
THE GREATEST QUEST

"This is how much God loved the world: He gave His Son, His one and only Son. And this is why: so that no one need be destroyed; by believing in Him, anyone can have a whole and lasting life. God didn't go to all the trouble of sending His Son merely to point an accusing finger, telling the world how bad it was. He came to help, to put the world right again. Anyone who trusts in Him is acquitted; anyone who refuses to trust Him has long since been under the death sentence without knowing it. And why? Because of that person's failure to believe in the one-of-a-kind Son of God when introduced to Him."

-John 3:16-18 MSG

When my son, Miguel was four years old, he was stung by a scorpion. At the time, our family lived in San Antonio, Texas; where I served as the worship pastor for a church. I was in my office when I got the call. Lucia told me that she and Miguel had already been to the doctor who had urged her to go to the hospital immediately. She called me en route to the Emergency Room. I was out of the building and in my car before we even finished the conversation.

By the time I arrived at the hospital, Miguel had been admitted. When I walked into his room, I was overwhelmed. I saw my little boy in a very big bed. The arm which had been stung was wrapped in big white gauze. His other arm lay limp with an IV running into it. He looked so helpless.

In that moment, I would've done anything to trade places with Miguel—I longed to take away the pain and fear he was experiencing. I would've gladly taken the sting and its horrible consequences to spare my son from all he went through. In the midst of those three days in the hospital, God allowed me to feel a tiny, dust speck of the weight He felt for Adam, Eve, and all of humanity.

As the first man and woman left the perfection of Eden, God already had a plan in place to put it right once again. God Himself would take humanity's place and bear the consequences of their disobedient decision. He was the only One who could afford to pay the price. Only a perfect, holy, and sinless life could restore the gravity of what had been lost.

God the Father would send His only Son, Jesus (not only a perfect reflection of God, but God Himself in the flesh) to bear the agonizing torment of a broken relationship and total separation from His Father. With Jesus as the One to pay the price of death, the owed debt of sin would be paid in full. By demonstrating

His immeasurable mercy towards us through Jesus, the perfect justice of God would be satisfied. Humanity could once again become reflections of God.

Jesus was the fulfillment of God's plan to restore His reflection in every man and every woman.

The shattered reflection can be restored. We don't have the power in and of ourselves to do it. It is impossible for us. But with Jesus as the God-man substitute—it can be done. When we stop putting faith in our fruitless attempts to shine on our own and accept what Jesus did on our behalf, He puts us together in a completely new way. We are restored to the original design God fashioned for Adam and Eve.

Jesus was the fulfillment of God's plan to restore His reflection in every man and every woman.

BIG IDEA

We can once again have a right relationship with Him and enact a meaningful responsibility to Him. Not because of anything we could ever do; humanity has already proven it to be impossible. It's all because of what Jesus has done. Simply accepting this fact is the key to becoming a new reflection of God.

This is why the Gospel is called, "Good News."

Years ago, I learned of a Japanese art form called "Kintsugi." When a potter makes a vase or a bowl, sometimes during the firing process the clay will shatter. The broken pieces are swept up but not thrown away. Instead of placing them into the garbage, the master potter gathers every broken shard. Next, he lovingly and painstakingly puts the vase or bowl back together. But here's the best part: the master doesn't simply glue it back together. He bonds every piece by filling the cracks with *gold*. When the vase or bowl is finished, every crack is evident and obvious because of the gold. It is now a breathtaking work of art. Even though it is completely restored, it is the brokenness which makes it unique and priceless. The gold between the shards makes it worth more than if it had never broken.

Just like the Kintsugi master, God takes our broken pieces and lovingly puts us together again. All those cracks in our lives can be filled by Jesus. All the pain, unforgiveness, anger, and betrayal which once held us captive can be removed by Jesus. Though it may take time for all areas of our brokenness to be healed—He promises to redeem our souls the instant we surrender to Him. Then, He walks alongside of us step-by-step, gently restoring all that we have lost.

In both instances, He is the gold that puts us back together. He doesn't hide our brokenness. He highlights it—revealing His work in the process. Since we all have broken uniquely, we are all uniquely restored.

It's the seams of gold which makes each one of us invaluable. Jesus paid the price for you and me to be restored once and for all. When the world sees what He has done for us, maybe they too will admit they are broken and allow Jesus to restore them.

The journey to the restoration humanity craves begins when an individual trusts Him. Each of us have the choice to let Him put us back together. Jesus said by simply believing, anyone can have a whole and lasting life.

This is how much God loved the world: He gave His Son, His one and only Son. And this is why: so that no one need be destroyed; by believing in Him, anyone can have a whole and lasting life. God didn't go to all the trouble of sending His Son merely to point an accusing finger, telling the world how bad it was. He came to help, to put the world right again. Anyone who trusts in Him is acquitted; anyone who refuses to trust Him has long since been under the death sentence without knowing it. And why? Because of that person's failure to believe in the one-of-a-kind Son of God when introduced to Him.

This is the crisis we're in: God-light streamed into the world, but men and women everywhere ran for the darkness. They went for the darkness because they were not really interested in pleasing God. Everyone who makes a practice of doing evil, addicted to denial and illusion, hates God-light and won't come near it, fearing a painful exposure. But anyone working and living in truth and reality welcomes God-light so the work can be seen for the God-work it is.

- John 3:16-21 MSG

God will always leave the choice up to you—just like He did for Adam and Eve. When you accept His gift of salvation through Jesus, you live out the unique reflection of His nature that you were created for. By walking in relationship *with* Him and responsibility *to* Him, you can live the quest you were uniquely designed to follow. Conversely, each individual has the freedom to reject trusting in Jesus and live apart from Him—shattered for all of eternity.

It comes down to this:

You cannot fulfill the quest God created you for if you are a shattered mirror.

No matter how many pieces you can hold in your hand, you'll never reflect God the way you were originally designed to. Relationship with and responsibility to Jesus is the only way for you to have the fullness God designed you to embody.

If you believe in Jesus and what He has done to restore His reflection in you, then I promise with absolute certainty that you are going to make a difference in this world beyond anything you can imagine.

Let me give you a final word of encouragement for this section: *You must have an incredible quest in front of you, because Jesus was willing to give His life so you could fulfill it.*

That's reason enough to keep moving forward.

Section Three

HEAR GOD CLEARLY

"My sheep hear My voice, and I know them, and they follow Me..." - Jesus; John 10:27 ESV

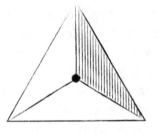

CHAPTER 10:
MISSING IT

"Do you see how they're missing it?" The sad tone of my friend's question possessed a hint of frustration. He shook his head in disappointment as he looked around at the guests standing in the queue.

An Imagineer friend of mine had invited me to ride a new and wildly popular Disney attraction with some of his other Imagineering friends. Imagineers are the people who actually dream, design, and build the amazing attractions Disney has a reputation for.

Though we could have avoided the line and boarded the attraction quickly, my friend chose to wait along with the park guests. Imagineers often do this to evaluate their work and future ways to "plus" an attraction to make it even better. They glean as much as possible from the guest perspective including what it feels like to stand in line, even if the wait time is a couple of hours.

As we waited, my friend leaned over to me and quietly pointed out how many guests were on their phones texting, reading social media, and posting photos. He couldn't believe how much of the experience around them was being overlooked. Disney Imagineers work incredibly hard to create a highly-detailed story for each and every attraction. The story begins to unfold even before you enter the queue. The storytelling becomes more and more detailed the closer you get to the loading zone.

My friend found it unfortunate how so many guests had missed out on the full experience (which, interestingly enough, they had paid a lot of money to see) because they were so distracted. They gave more attention to their devices than they did absorbing the moment which had been created for their enjoyment.

I wonder how often we, as followers of Jesus, do the same? How often are we oblivious to what Jesus is actually doing?

He is at work all around us, waiting for us to jump in and partner with Him. Could it be we are so distracted by little things that we miss out on the things which really matter—even though they are right in front of us?

When we launched Cast Member Church, I quickly discovered a pattern among young Christians who wanted to help us get it started. They had three things in common:

1.   *They didn't know how to recognize when God was speaking to them.*

2.   *They were afraid to live their faith in a way which was plainly visible.*

3.   *They had little to no Kingdom Influence in the world around them.*

One young lady stands out in my memory. She grew up in a Christian home, attended a Christian school (K through 12), and graduated from a Christian university. After getting to know us for a while, she seemed put off by our church's mission. She sat down with me and told me she didn't believe she was called to make disciples. She didn't feel Jesus' "Great Commission" applied to her.

Jesus, undeterred, went right ahead and gave His charge: "God authorized and commanded Me to commission you: Go out and train everyone you meet, far and near, in this way of life, marking them by baptism in the threefold name: Father, Son, and Holy Spirit. Then instruct them in the practice of all I have commanded you. I'll be with you as you do this, day after day after day, right up to the end of the age.

Matthew 28:18-20 MSG

I was truly puzzled by her words. I wasn't even sure how to respond. Lucia and I had gotten to know her pretty well over the course of several weeks. We had been happy to find she had an amazing grasp of the Bible. Her knowledge of Scripture was impressive. I didn't understand how she reached her conclusion to be exempted from one of the most important commands in the entire Bible.

The more I thought about it, I realized what caused her to make such a glaring misstatement. In all of her Christian experience and equipping opportunities, she had never been taught how to live out her faith in the real world.

More importantly, she didn't know how to transform the knowledge she gained over the years into action.

This wasn't her fault. No one had walked beside her, giving her a living example to follow. No one had patiently and graciously modeled for her how to hear God's voice with clarity, follow His lead with courage, and have Kingdom Influence to the world in which she worked. She had been educated, but she had never been mentored. No one had ever walked with her, modeling what it looked like to make a disciple. *No wonder she didn't think she could make disciples.* She had missed out on a huge part of the adventure which she had been created for and it broke my heart.

From that day forward, I committed to do two things:

1.   *To not just make disciples, but to raise up a movement of "Disciplemakers."*

2.   *To develop a simple tool to help those within the movement to find the clarity, courage, and confidence necessary to become Kingdom Influencers for the rest of their lives.*

Because we have held to these commitments, Cast Member Church established a reputation for our expanding Disciplemaking culture.

The Quest Compass has become our core discipling tool, providing a simple framework to help anyone grow as a disciple of Jesus, as well as become a healthy, reproducing Disciplemaker. If those in our church are learning to hear God clearly, follow Jesus courageously, and light their world confidently—we know they can be a powerful force for the Kingdom of God. The Quest Compass has made that possible.

Over the next few chapters, I'm going to share with you the same exact framework we share with those who are part of Cast Member Church. It is my desire for you to experience the same adventure we are experiencing here at Walt Disney World. I want you to enjoy the same fruitfulness we see in the areas of Kingdom movement, momentum, and multiplication.

God is ready to reveal to you the quest He has created you for. It begins by laying aside distractions and investing the time to pay attention.

BIG IDEA

You are about to learn how to recognize God's voice when He *calls* you, how to move forward through the *challenges* which will inevitably oppose your call and interpret the *changes* God is stirring up as a result of your obedience.

The Quest Compass will help you to apply Scripture to your life like never before. It will make you aware of God's involvement in the smallest details and daily tasks. You will sense Him sitting with you in the coffee house as you talk with a friend. You will be aware of His presence as you walk through the grocery store. You will grow familiar with His nearness at work or in the classroom.

The Quest Compass will help you process as you pray for guidance.

God's voice will become so familiar that you'll discover the beautiful intimacy of His presence with you at all times.

God is ready to reveal to you the quest He has created you for. It begins by laying aside distractions and investing the time to pay attention. It won't be long before you will step into the adventure He has fashioned just for you. He works out details most people will miss, but you won't. You will see Him at work and be equipped to point out to others what He is really up to.

One simple word of encouragement/warning: Once you pass this point of the book, there's no going back. What you are about to read will stay with you for the rest of your life. Everything is about to change. My prayer is for you to invest in His leading in such a way that you are forever changed. You'll look back one day and be glad you kept moving forward. You'll be amazed at how far you will have come...

...and you won't have missed anything God was doing along the way.

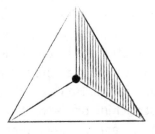

CHAPTER 11:
DISCERNING GOD'S VOICE

One hot summer day, a farmer loaded bales of hay into his barn. He spent all day carrying in every bale, stacking them until they reached from the barn floor to the highest beam. Feeling exhausted yet content from the day's work, he came into the house and sat down with his family for dinner.

As he folded his hands, preparing to give thanks to God for the food, he glanced at his wrist. Suddenly, he realized his watch was missing. It had fallen off at some point while he stacked the bales. His son, seeing his father's face and knowing how precious the watch was to him, was moved to act.

"I can find it for you, Dad."

"No son," the father replied, thinking about the enormity of the suggestion. "There's no way you can find it. It's long gone."

Determined to find the watch, the boy waited until dinner was finished and snuck out to the barn. He climbed up to top of the stack and laid down on his back. He then closed his eyes and didn't move a muscle. He took long, deep breaths and listened. He could hear the creaks and pops of the barn as the evening breeze blew against its wooden frame. He listened more intently. He heard a mouse scratching on the crossbeam. He held his breath. All he could hear was the thumping of his heart.

As time passed and his heart settled, he felt one with the hay. Then, ever so faintly, he heard it.

Tick...tick...tick...tick.

He turned his head slowly, attempting to focus deep into the stack.

He got up and moved a few bales. Once again, he laid down, waited, and focused.

Tick...tick...tick...tick.

Over and over he got up, moved bales, and then lay still to listen intently.

Tick...tick...tick...tick.

An hour or so later, the boy ran back to the house. He proudly handed his father the lost watch.

His father was elated *and* quite curious.

"How on earth did you find it?"

The boy smiled at his father and said, "I just had to be still. The watch did the rest."

The Lord said, "Go out and stand on the mountain in the presence of the Lord, for the Lord is about to pass by." Then a great and powerful wind tore the mountains apart and shattered the rocks before the Lord, but the Lord was not in the wind. After the wind there was an earthquake, but the Lord was not in the earthquake. After the earthquake came a fire, but the Lord was not in the fire.

And after the fire came a gentle whisper.

- 1 Kings 19:11,12 NIV

Let's admit that when we think about God speaking to us, we imagine it happens in some dramatic fashion. Who wouldn't want to see a burning bush, a hand writing on a wall, an angel bearing tidings of great joy or hear a booming voice from heaven? This is how most people imagine it would be like to hear from God. Don't get me wrong; those moments can happen. Yet, I believe God takes great joy in communicating with us in an even more powerful way: *a conversation.*

A relationship with God is designed to run two ways. It's close. It's honest. It's meaningful. It's unique to the two of you. It goes beyond two people passing on the street, exchanging momentary pleasantries. This kind of conversation is much better. It's you and God working through the stuff of life; the stuff which really matters.

You talk and He listens.
He talks and you listen.

Sometimes neither of you talk because simply being together is enough.

God, your loving Daddy, doesn't send you out on your quest alone. He goes with you every step of the way. As a dad myself, I can tell you I love walking with my children. We have the best conversations about everything you could imagine. God wants to do the same with you. That's what dads do.

"But how do you know when God is actually speaking to you?"

I hear this question often. It's a fair question. If we are going to act based on what God says, we need to make sure it is of Him and not of our own imaginations. I welcome and celebrate this question because it highlights the fact you want to be accountable to His leading.

In order for you to know for sure when God is calling you, you have to *DISCERN* His voice from all the other voices around you and within you.

God could choose to speak to you in an infinite number of ways. If He wanted to speak to you in an audible voice, He could. I have several friends who have heard God speak with a voice they heard with their physical ears. Their stories are fascinating and quite encouraging. I don't consider any of my friends to be mentally unstable, rather I respect how God leads them. I'm aware most of us have not had the benefit of hearing God speak audibly. But, it doesn't mean He won't. He's God and He can speak however He chooses.

For most of us, God's leading comes in a *still, small voice.*

We must learn to "tune" our quests to three distinct "frequencies" on which God speaks. The more we learn *how* He speaks, the more we will be able to *DISCERN* what He is saying every time He speaks. You'll be surprised to find He speaks more often than you think.

We can rest confident in His voice as we come to understand how He speaks:

1. God speaks through His Word (the Bible).
2. God speaks through prayer.
3. God speaks through wise counsel.

If you have followed Jesus for any length of time, these ways to hear Him are familiar. However, don't take your current understanding of them for granted. Each contain a wealth of access to God's heart and mind. Scripture, prayer, and wise counsel—both individually and collectively—make God's voice clearly known in any given situation.

 BIG IDEA For most of us, God's leading comes in a still, small voice.

If you want to recognize God's voice in your life, it is imperative to focus through the cacophony of your busyness and listen intently for the tick...tick...tick...tick of His calling. Scripture, prayer, and wise counsel will tune your heart to hear it.

In the course of time, you'll easily recognize His gentle whisper simply by stilling yourself and letting Him do the rest.

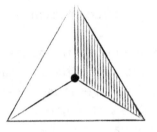

CHAPTER 12:
Hearing God's Voice in the Bible

By your words I can see where I'm going; they throw a beam of light on my dark path.

- Psalm 119:105 MSG

There's a video floating around the Internet that melts my heart every time I see it. It's of a group of underground Believers in China receiving Bibles for the very first time. They respectfully unwrap the plastic which seals the Bible. They caress the cover as if it was a newborn baby. The video pans across their faces as they open their Bibles. As they look through the pages of God's Word in their own language, you can see the look of awe and wonder on their faces.

It isn't long before tears begin to fall freely from their eyes. In the midst of their joyful weeping, they begin to pray, giving thanks to God that they are able to hold His words in their hands. Many hug their Bibles as if they were hugging Jesus Himself. They know they are endangering their very lives just for having a Bible in their possession. For them, it doesn't matter because the words on those sacred pages mean more than life.

I spend much of my time with younger people from all over the world who have little to no understanding of God or the Bible. Their ages range generally between 18 to 30 years old. The vast majority of them have never owned a Bible, nor have they ever read one. It's not for their lack of access to one or even opposition to it. It's just they've never felt the need to open a Bible.

Followers of Jesus believe the Bible is the revelation of God. It is how He chose to make Himself known to you, me, and the rest of the world. It's His autobiography, told through the words of kings, commoners, criminals, poets, and prophets. It opens a world beyond what is seen with human eyes while also speaking into the routines and realities of everyday life. The Bible is the authority over all which is, has been, and ever will be.

It is God's Word.

If we are to know and follow the quest God has designed each of us to live, the Bible is our source to understand what our quests will look like. Because it is timeless and applicable to any person or situation, the Bible can speak directly to us about:

Our thoughts and actions.
Our jobs and career directions.
Our families and friends.
Our hopes and dreams.
Our doubts, fears, and regrets.
Every aspect of life we can possibly experience.

If we are to learn how God speaks to us, we must explore the pages of the Bible to discover how He has already spoken to those who have gone before us. Because God never changes, we have an opportunity to see—through His revealed Word—who He is, how He interacts with those who follow Him, and what our response should be.

The Bible is God's autobiography, told through the words of kings, commoners, criminals, poets, and prophets. **BIG IDEA**

The Bible is God's MANIFESTO.

Everything God wants us to know about Himself is contained between the covers of Scripture. His unconditional love, uncompromising truth, unblemished righteousness, unfathomable mercy, and unimaginable grace flow through every page from Genesis 1 to Revelation 22.

We know when He speaks to us, He cannot lie, change, or contradict what He has already stated in the Bible. His Word is the litmus test for what He says to us, how He speaks to us, and wherever He might lead us. When we sense His calling in our lives—telling us to go here or do that—the Bible must confirm such a calling, otherwise the calling is not from God.

When you sense God speaking to you through a sense, feeling, perception, or picture—never hesitate to ask yourself, "Has God said or done this before?" Is there a place in Scripture where something similar happened to someone else? If you can identify something similar in the Bible, and that section of verses aligns with the complete message of the Bible as a whole (meaning we don't take verses out of context), don't be surprised to find you're hearing God speak to you.

The Bible is God's MIRROR.

The Bible opens our spiritual eyes for us to see ourselves and the world around us from God's perspective. It also exposes our sinful nature which led to our brokenness.

God's Word reminds us no one has it all together and therefore we are unable to boast in our own goodness. Apart from Him, there is nothing good in us. The Bible as a mirror, makes it clear how much we need Him.

This mirror also reveals how God sees us through the filter of His Son and that even in our sinful nature, He loved us. Because Jesus was willing to be broken in our place, paying our debt for our rebellion, the Bible shows us how we are made right through Him. We are restored and can trust Him to guide us in every aspect of our lives.

When we read the Bible, we are assured He is working with us, appointing us as His ambassadors to the world. Because the Bible tells us God is our Daddy and King, we can courageously follow Him as His children, bearing His authority.

The Bible is God's MAP.

God's Word reveals the geography of His Kingdom. It's not a physical landscape consisting of nations or borders assigned by men. It is a distribution of powers and authorities. The Bible guides us as we move about this topography, amidst what we can see and more importantly, what we cannot see.

The Bible makes known who is working against us. It reveals to us how the Enemy has operated since the dawn of time. Scripture shows us how to overcome dark powers which attempt to subvert our God-given quests. Throughout the Word, you can see numerous men and women who have encountered such opposition. Their experiences challenge us to learn from each of their quests and apply them to our own.

The Bible reveals how God works for our good. It shares how we may depend upon Him to lead us through to the fulfillment of our quests. We are assured time and time again that we are never alone. We have absolutely no reason to fear anything which might come against us. We can read quest after quest within the Biblical narrative of multiple times in which God provided and protected those who chose to follow Him and live out their quest with faith.

The Word of God also shows us where the history of mankind is headed. We are shown the end for a good reason. The last book of the Bible, Revelation, gives us a hope and future we can claim today. It reminds us this broken world is not our final home. Our present hard times cannot compare to the good coming when God sets everything right once and for all.

Such perspective encourages us to make the most of today, bringing His light into the lives of those around us. Every man, woman, and child needs a hope and a future that only God can give them! Because the Bible reveals the future of humanity, it's like we've already seen the end of the movie. We know it's amazing and we are inspired to help others share in the same joy.

God speaks to us through the Bible to assure us of His voice. Knowing His ways and how He has spoken to humanity throughout history gives us insight into how and when He speaks to us. Resting secure in this knowledge of His character, we recognize Him immediately. The more time we spend reading His Word, the clearer His voice becomes. When God is doing something around us, we are able to easily distinguish it. How? Because we have seen Him do the same throughout the pages of Scripture.

It doesn't take a Bible scholar to interpret God's call. It just takes someone who knows Him well enough to recognize when He is calling. The Bible is the place to start because on those pages—His voice and words are clear.

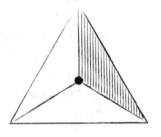

CHAPTER 13:
HEARING GOD'S
VOICE IN PRAYER

"Don't bargain with God. Be direct. Ask for what you need. This isn't a cat-and-mouse, hide-and-seek game we're in. If your child asks for bread, do you trick him with sawdust? If he asks for fish, do you scare him with a live snake on his plate? As bad as you are, you wouldn't think of such a thing. You're at least decent to your own children. So don't you think the God who conceived you in love will be even better?"
- Jesus (Matthew 7:7-11) MSG

"I don't believe in the power of prayer. I believe in the power of Jesus, so I ask for His help a lot." - Pete Greig

---

"How do you pray?"

I didn't think it was a difficult question until the only answer I heard was silence. The small group of young people sitting with me at the Tomorrowland Terrace at Magic Kingdom just stared at me. It was obvious none had ever been asked this question before. I asked, not to belittle them in any way, but to open up a dialogue about what held them back or what confusions they might have. As the sun began to set behind Cinderella Castle, we engaged in the most amazing conversation. Here is how I would summarize each of their responses:

"I really don't know how to pray."
"I've never seen a prayer make any difference."
"I'm afraid to pray."

Pay close attention to those statements. None of them said they didn't believe in prayer. The common theme surrounded a lack of understanding what prayer really is. They are not alone. The majority of followers of Jesus lack a depth of understanding when it comes to prayer. They might not admit it openly, but when the surface is scratched it doesn't take long for the admission to be exposed. It is time for us to openly and freely admit it. Stating confusions or hesitations does not equate to lack of belief—rather it provides room to be discipled and grow.

Prayer is oxygen to a life-giving relationship with God. Our journey cannot survive without it. I know this for sure: if a follower of Jesus lacks Kingdom Influence, it is because they lack a passion for prayer. This does not mean they are not passionate people—it simply means the passion is not first directed towards God's leading of that passion.

If this is you, you are not alone. I'm not criticizing, condemning, or looking down on you. I believe you likely were never given an opportunity to be mentored in the area of prayer.

Could it be possible you feel a little (or a lot) like the ones to whom I asked the question of prayer? Do their honest responses resonate with something you may be feeling?

Maybe you've never learned how to pray.

Maybe you've never seen your prayers make a tangible difference.

Maybe you've felt afraid to pray for some reason.

God wants to be with you, guide you, and empower you for the unique quest He has designed for you. For those very reasons, I find it extremely hard to believe He would make prayer a difficult thing. I believe the complete opposite:

God wants prayer to be the easiest thing you could ever do.

Think about it this way: I can be in a crowded room and still know my wife's voice from all of the others. She's not a loud talker like I am. But she does have this amazing—dare I say—sexy, Mexican accent. I know her voice anywhere because I know who she is and what her voice sounds like. I also know the things she would and wouldn't say. The Bible is similar; it helps us to recognize God's voice. It gives insight into who God is, what His voice sounds like, and what He would and wouldn't say.

Here is my simple definition of prayer:

A conversation with God.

You thought I was going to say something profound. You might have been expecting some kind of amazing wisdom you would have to ponder for days. Sorry to disappoint you.

A conversation with God is simply *talking to Him and listening to Him.*

Most people I encounter think prayer means talking to God and hoping for the best outcome—as if we say it and then something may or may not magically happen. They see prayer as a one-way conversation. They ask God for "stuff" like blessings, forgiveness, protection, etc. They never expect a response.

It isn't wrong to ask for things from God. Jesus said we could ask for anything in His name. However, prayer is so much more than just asking God for things. As a parent, I can tell you if my kids were to only ask me for things (even the important stuff), and not be interested in a conversation, I'd be very disappointed. God is a relational being. He wants for there to be dialogue and meaningful exchange.

 BIG IDEA Prayer is about sharing openly and having God involved in every moment of your life—the hard, the wonderful, the scary, and the exhilarating.

So, how do we talk to God?

The simple answer is you talk to God the same way you talk to your spouse or best friend. Be yourself. Be honest. He knows everything about you already. But know this, I believe He has the biggest smile in His face when He gets to hear from you about what you are thinking and feeling. We all know how important it is when someone tells us something vulnerable, even if we already know. It was special because they trusted us enough to say it to out loud in a meaningful moment. You can't fool God. So, just start talking with the understanding there is absolutely nothing you can hide.

Prayer is about sharing openly and having God involved in every moment in your life—the hard, the wonderful, the scary, and the exhilarating. We invite Him in into our hopes, dreams, failures, and heartaches. He invites us to understand Him and His ways. We form a deep connection with our Creator. He walks and talks with us through every stage of our journey.

Talk out loud if you can.

When you pray out loud, you have to really think through what you are saying. Thoughts can easily wander when we talk to God in our head. He hears those thoughts and there's nothing wrong with this practice, especially when you are around other people who might not understand what you're doing.

Pray out loud if you're alone in the car. Don't worry about what others might think. All the other drivers will think you are singing with the radio or talking to someone via hands-free mode on your mobile.

Talking to God means telling Him about what's going on in your life. Tell Him about your day; about the highs and the lows. Tell Him about the frustrations and the funny stuff. He loves it. Tell Him about what is bothering you or scaring you. Just tell Him what's going on and how you're feeling.

Let Him know you need Him. Like I said, it's okay to ask for things. He is a Giver of good gifts. If you're feeling afraid of something, ask Him for protection. If you're worried about your finances, ask Him for provision. If you are concerned about a friend's health, ask for healing. He loves you and He loves it when you come to Him with whatever is on your heart.

Just don't let this be where you stop. Many people present their petition to God and figure it's in His hands now. But God wants to enjoy a conversation with you. He wants to talk as well. As we quiet ourselves, we learn how to listen to His voice. As I've said before, I don't necessarily mean an audible voice, but you can still hear Him if you know how to listen from the inward place.

How do we learn to listen to God?

Listening requires stillness and patience. Of course, if God wants to speak right away, He will. However, He often wants us to wait on His voice. He has a very good reason. He desires for us to be near Him. So, He will wait until we still ourselves. Sometimes He takes His time so we draw as close as we can to Him. Why? Because sometimes just His nearness is the answer.

When He does speak, you will recognize His voice in three subtle, yet powerful ways:

1.   **You will feel it in your GUT.**
2.   **It will be GOOD.**
3.   **It will be for His GLORY.**

You will feel it in your GUT.

Many people refer to hearing God in their "heart of hearts." It's the place where you feel butterflies when you are nervous. It comes from the place you experience the joy of falling in love. It is where you can feel deep empathy for another's pain. The Bible describes Jesus as having felt this:

When He saw the crowds, He had compassion on them, because they were harassed and helpless, like sheep without a shepherd. - Matthew 9:36 NIV

The word "compassion" comes from a Greek word σπλαγχνίζομαι or "splagchnizomai" meaning to "feel it in one's inward parts." Some Bible commentaries refer to it as "the twisting of the intestines." I know that's rather graphic, but now you know.

When you feel it in your gut, there's a good chance it is God who is speaking. Just know, this is not the only filter to DISCERN through. Our hearts can deceive us in our emotions, which lie close to the gut. This is why we DISCERN by comparing what we believe we hear to what is in Scripture. Next, we move to two more steps.

It will be GOOD.

God's plans are always good and never for harm. Whatever He is saying will line up with His Word. When the apostle Paul tells us to ponder the things of God, they are always good. As you are discerning God's voice, Paul's words could apply as well:

...whatever is true, whatever is noble, whatever is right, whatever is pure, whatever is lovely, whatever is admirable—if anything is excellent or praiseworthy—think about such things.

- Philippians 4:8 NIV

It will be for God's GLORY.

In other words, God will get the credit, not you. Here's how Jesus said it:

...let your light shine before others, that they may see your good deeds and glorify your Father in heaven.

– Jesus; Matthew 5:16 NIV

It can be very tempting to do good with the motive of looking good in front of others. We have to be vigilant to *DISCERN* what God is saying versus what we want to hear. Sometimes God will tell you, in your gut, to do something good, but you might end up looking foolish. You could perceive His leading as not "good" because it isn't "good" for you. Unfortunately, I have lots of experience with this one. Truth is, it stings to write it.

If God is speaking to you, you will feel it in your *GUT* (your heart of hearts), you will know it is *GOOD* (the Bible confirms it's the right thing to do), and God will get the *GLORY* (God is the One who receives credit).

As we learn to converse with God, His voice will become so clear that we will hear Him all the time. I like to joke with people that once you understand how to recognize God's voice, you'll discover He rarely is silent. I mean this to be an encouraging thing. I say it, because I believe God has a sense of humor and laughs with me. I've learned this many times in my conversations with Him.

God is always ready to listen, speak, and even laugh as we're willing to take the time to have an ongoing conversation with Him.

Prayer can, and should become, the most important part of your life. The good news is, you have all the time in the world to confidently practice it as you learn who God is, what He sounds like, and what He would and would not say. Such clarity provides you the security to have absolute trust, however and wherever He leads you.

By the way, I'm certain He's available to chat right now.

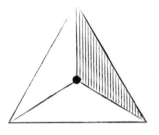

CHAPTER 14:
HEARING GOD'S VOICE
IN WISE COUNSEL

By yourself you're unprotected. With a friend you can face the worst. Can you round up a third? A three-stranded rope isn't easily snapped.

- Ecclesiastes 4:12 MSG

When two of you get together on anything at all on earth and make a prayer of it, my Father in heaven goes into action. And when two or three of you are together because of Me, you can be sure that I'll be there."

- (Jesus) Matthew 18:19,20 MSG

Every adventurer has a mentor.

> Luke Skywalker had Obi Wan Kenobi.
> Pinocchio had Jiminy Cricket.
> Cinderella had the Fairy Godmother.
> Frodo had Gandalf.
> Scarlett O'Hara had Melanie Wilkes.

Every story you've ever seen or read includes someone who plays the role of the wiser, level-headed sage who knows more of the story than the hero. The mentor guides the protagonist to a place of self-discovery. This relationship is vital to the story. Even Tom Hanks' character in *Cast Away* invented a mentor of sorts with a volleyball he named, "Wilson."

Every quest requires a mentor. Your quest is no different. You need someone in your life to help you process if, how, what, and why God is speaking to you.

The Bible is filled with numerous mentoring relationships:

> Jethro mentored Moses.
> Samuel mentored David.
> Naomi mentored Ruth.
> Elizabeth mentored Mary.
> Barnabas mentored Paul.
> Paul mentored Timothy.

These relationships are evidence of the emphasis the Bible places on seeking out wise counsel.

Take good counsel and accept correction—that's the way to live wisely and well. We humans keep brainstorming options and plans, but God's purpose prevails.

- Proverbs 19:20,21 MSG

God has not designed us to pursue our quests on our own. He wants us to look to each other to encourage and be encouraged. He desires for us to challenge and be challenged by each other. As we seek wise counsel, it becomes an amazing way for us to recognize God's voice.

First, I want to tell you what wise counsel isn't.

Wise counsel is not an opinion. It isn't prefaced with the statement, "Well, if I were you—here's what I would do...." Wise counsel does not impose a personal position formed by preference. Preference is about what someone thinks, not what God says.

Wise counsel is not cheerleading. It doesn't agree with everything said simply because it wants you to succeed. It doesn't say "yes" because it wants you to be happy. Cheerleading can be an insincere form of encouragement. Sometimes encouragement has to challenge you in order for God's voice to become clear.

Wise counsel is not nitpicking. It doesn't make you feel as if everything you are doing is wrong. It doesn't quibble or find fault. This is simply a critical attitude and certainly doesn't help you to *DISCERN* God's voice.

The heart of wise counsel leads you to know if God is the source of what you hear or not. Having someone in your life who can be supportive, and at the same time objective, allows you to develop a keen sense of discernment.

Wise counsel comes from those you trust.

These individuals share an understanding that God speaks to those who are willing to listen and leads those who choose to follow. These mentors look to Scripture and pray over the same issues as you. They are invested in your quest. They seek to be a part of your growth as a disciple.

Wise counsel stems from those who can be honest with you.

They have the freedom to speak freely. You don't feel threatened because you know they have the same objective in mind; to ask, seek, and knock with the expectation of a Divine response. When they don't share the same conclusion as you do about what God is saying, you are willing to weigh their perspective as much as your own.

Wise counsel comes from those who believe in you.

As I said earlier, they are not cheerleaders; but it doesn't mean they don't support you. On the contrary, they want to see God move in and through your life as much as you do. They approach you with encouragement. When they believe God is behind what you are hearing, no one will be more excited than these individuals.

Faith and foolishness look incredibly similar to those who don't know you. God could be leading you into something which might appear crazy to most people. A person of wise counsel stands with you if they believe God is up to something, even if it may seem unconventional and out of the ordinary.

Wise counsel is best cultivated in a discipling/ mentoring relationship.

Having someone who is committed to help you grow in the character and competencies of Jesus will make all the difference. They will be keenly aware of the good, the bad, and the ugly in you. They will also see Jesus at work in your life. For this reason, they will be your best source of encouragement and challenge.

God has not designed us to pursue our quests on our own. He wants us to look to each other to encourage and be encouraged.

When wise counsel, Scripture, and prayer come together to clarify what God is saying, you can be assured His voice will become less of a distant echo or hunch. Instead, you will know with certainty that you can depend on it every time you hear it.

Discerning God's voice isn't difficult. Don't let others make it difficult. It takes practice and there will be times you get it wrong. But that's how you learn and improve. Be humble and ready for the next time. God wants you to hear His voice more than you do.

Keep listening.

If you think you're hearing His voice, there's one more way to identify if it's Him for sure. You simply need to take a deep breath and turn the page.

God's call is about to get a little dangerous.

Section Four

FACE THE UNKNOWN

Trust in the Lord with all your heart, and do not lean on your own understanding. Proverbs 3:5 NIV

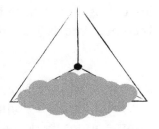

CHAPTER 15:
EMBRACING THE DARE

In all my years immersed in the Disney culture, I've observed what could easily be over a million guests in the parks. I have seen the absolute best and admittedly worst displays of humanity. In it all, I have come to a startling conclusion. Regardless of ethnicity, gender, religion, socio-economic status, or political affiliation—I believe only two kinds of people exist in this world:

Those who like to ride Space Mountain
—and those who don't.

Here's my case and point:

One day while walking through Magic Kingdom, I noticed the wait time was unusually short for the queue to Space Mountain. Some might be tempted to believe that as the leader of a church based in the heart of Walt Disney World, I ride the attractions all the time.

They would be wrong.

In fact, I rarely ride unless I am looking to connect with a specific Cast Member who is working in a specific attraction.

On this particular day, I was at Magic Kingdom for a meeting. As I walked through Tomorrowland, the futuristic warbles of the atmospheric music filled the air. I noticed an unusually short queue at Space Mountain. The sign above the entrance indicated a 20-minute wait for the stand-by queue; a rare occasion indeed. I glanced at my watch and realized I happened to have some extra time before my meeting. Thinking it might be nice to get out of the Florida heat and enjoy a quick trip around the universe, I entered the queue.

Just inside the entrance, I passed a sign telling potential riders what to expect:

"Space Mountain is a thrilling, high speed, turbulent rollercoaster-type ride in the dark that includes sharp turns, sudden drops, and stops. For safety, you should be in good health and free from high blood pressure, heart, back, or neck problems, motion sickness, or other conditions that could be aggravated by this adventure."

Right behind me came a husband and wife. They were perhaps 10 years older than me. She carried a bright blue "Disney Parks" bag of souvenirs in one hand. Her other hand tightly gripped her husband's forearm. The husband definitely showed more excitement about riding Space Mountain than his wife did. She made it plainly known that she didn't want to venture into an unknown escapade of twisting and turning through the darkness of space.

At first, all I could hear were low conversational tones from both of them. I heard the husband assure his wife she would have a good time. He attempted to alleviate her anxiety with promises such as, "It's gonna be okay, baby. Trust me, you're gonna love it." She didn't seem convinced.

As the queue reached the convergence point in which you pass the rocket-like ride vehicles preparing to launch, the woman's fear intensified. The conversation between them grew more audible.

"I don't think I'm gonna make it," the woman said with great hesitation.

"Baby, do you trust me?" came the husband's reply.

They went back and forth like this for the rest of the twenty-minute wait. I pretended to not notice their conversation. By the time we arrived at the loading zone, however, everyone else within earshot was quite aware of the growing stress between them.

The loading Cast Member asked how many were in my party. I held up one finger to let her know it was just me. As I boarded the front of the vehicle, I realized the couple had been given the two seats behind mine since the vehicle capacity is designed for three riders. Knowing how much commotion had already occurred in the queue, I thought to myself, albeit sarcastically:

"This will be fun."

The wife gripped her bag tightly. She hesitated before she boarded. Her husband offered reassuring words before she stepped into the vehicle. She plopped down in the seat directly behind me, stowed her bag, and pulled the safety T-bar into position. Unconvinced of its design, I heard her tug the bar repeatedly to make sure it was doing its job. A Cast Member checked our restraints, offered a friendly Disney wave, and we were off.

Our vehicle dipped ever so slightly and began to move up the long track where we would be dropped from our launch position. Blue lights pulsated past us as we entered the launch tunnel. The further up the track we traveled, the faster the blue lights flashed, staged to create the sensation of preparing to be shot into space. Music and techno sound effects charged the immersive atmosphere. But above it all—I heard this woman behind me half-praying. Maybe it was chanting. I honestly couldn't tell.

"Ooooohhhh, Jesus, Jesus, Jesus, Jesus, Jesus, Jesus, Je-sus."

She drew a long breath.

"Ooooohhhh, Jesus, Jesus, Jesus, Jesus, Jesus, Jesus, Je-sus."

She sucked in another deep breath.

"Ooooohhhh...."

This repeated all the way to the top.

Our vehicle leveled off and I anticipated the drop—half because of the experience I knew was coming, and half because I was honestly curious what would happen with this woman.

I'm not sure if I can adequately describe what took place next.

As our vehicle plunged into the darkness, this woman released a bloodcurdling scream which rings in my ears to this day. But this was not all. The scream was only a prelude for what was to come. For the entire length of the ride, this woman dedicated and rededicated her life to God.

"Oh Lord, save me!"

"AHHHHHHHHHHHHHHHH!"

"Jesus, help me!"

"AHHHHHHHHHHHHHHHHH!"

"Oh God, I don't wanna die!"

"Jesus, have mercy!"

Finally, with the grace of a great brake system, we returned from our trip into space and came to an abrupt stop at the loading dock. I looked back to make sure the woman was still alive. She was, but she stared off—not saying anything for some reason. Her husband helped her out of the vehicle. He timidly said, "You see, that *was* fun."

I found it odd how she didn't respond. She gathered the bag and charged past her husband through the merchandise shop and out into the sunlight. I trailed behind, somewhat surprised she had gone mute. As her husband caught up to her, she suddenly and without warning, swung her bag of souvenirs and hit her husband across the back of his head.

I needed to get to my meeting, but I figured the next few minutes could prove to be incredibly entertaining. I am embarrassed to admit I decided to watch to see what would happen.

What came next—I find disturbing to this day.

From the same mouth which only moments ago had confessed Jesus and called upon Him for mercy, came a string of vulgarities which could melt letters off the Space Mountain sign.

"How dare you take me on that ------- ride!"

"Were you trying to ---------- kill me?"

"You ------------!"

People ducked behind benches, tables, and chairs. Parents grabbed their children and ran for cover.

Okay, so the ducking and hiding didn't happen; but the incident certainly caught everyone's attention. You could tell it disturbed more than just parents of small children. Her reaction was unbecoming and to be honest—shocking.

The woman cursed her husband. She cursed Space Mountain. She cursed Disney. She may have even cursed Mickey Mouse. Such a colorful display of language would've even made Joe Pesci blush.

The rabid woman walked off with her husband toward Fantasyland. Those in the vicinity gave the couple a wide berth. I shook my head and headed in the direction of my meeting.

My observation of humanity had been confirmed:

There are those who like to ride Space Mountain and those who don't.

While the woman's behavior was inexcusable, the truth is—she proved a point. Each one of us approaches the unknown differently. Treading into the unfamiliar is not something many of us enjoy. We do our best to avoid it if at all possible. But when it comes to the quest God has created each of us for, we must expect to go beyond what is familiar and comfortable.

This unfamiliarity is the second "D" of The Quest Compass. We move from simple hearing or *discerning* God's voice towards an actionable step He reveals to us. This is what I call the "*DARE*."

DISCERN and *DARE* are the bookends of the call of God. To know for sure if you hear Him clearly, you should anticipate a *DARE*. There wasn't anyone in all of Scripture who wasn't confronted with some sort of *DARE* paired with God's call.

The same is true for us. There will be an action God will ask us to take in response to His leading. Whatever that action is, it will lead us into some kind of challenge.

That's why it's a *DARE*.

To fulfill your quest, you have to be willing to go beyond the familiar. A *DARE* leads you into unfamiliar territory. It grows your faith.

This is where the extraordinary happens.

Embracing the *DARE* requires trust. It requires us to depend upon God—His leadership, His direction, His provision, and His protection.

Whatever challenge God has called you to face, it will be impossible to face it apart from Him.

It doesn't matter how talented, gifted, strong, or passionate you are. Your quest will require His partnership. He will use things like your talents and gifts. After all, He gave them to you. But those alone will not accomplish His purpose for your life. He wants you to lean on Him throughout the course of your quest instead of trying in vain to rely upon yourself.

Whatever challenge God has called you to face, it will be impossible to face it apart from Him. **BIG IDEA**

Like the woman on Space Mountain, you can scream at the unknown. You have a choice in how you respond to the thrills and twists which happen in the dark spaces of life. The truth is, it may feel extremely scary to think about the invisible Jesus leading you beyond what is familiar. But there is another option. You can embrace the unknown. You can move from just *hearing* Him in the *DISCERN* stage and expectantly look for the *DARE*.

By embracing the *DARE*, I guarantee you can be launched into a quest which makes following Jesus a thrilling adventure. It will come with ups and downs, sudden turns, and darkened unknowns—but anticipating and accepting it will bring fulfillment into your life like never before.

You will experience God's presence at every turn, guaranteeing plot twists which rival any movie you have ever seen.

CHAPTER 16:
DOUBT, FEAR, AND REGRET

Jesus didn't hesitate. He reached down and grabbed His hand. Then He said, "Faint-heart, what got into you?"

- Matthew 14:31 MSG

Light, space, zest—that's God! So, with Him on my side I'm fearless, afraid of no one and nothing.

- Psalm 27:1 MSG

God's loyal love couldn't have run out, His merciful love couldn't have dried up. They're created new every morning. How great your faithfulness! I'm sticking with God (I say it over and over). He's all I've got left.

- Lamentations - 3:23,24 MSG

As you *DISCERN* God's call and contemplate the *DARE* He places before you, it is certain you'll encounter opposition from the start. It will come from the serpent who kept Adam and Eve from thriving in their God-given quests. He is now focused on you. The thought of you moving forward into your God-given quest infuriates him, so he releases his weapons in your direction. Interesting note—these are the same weapons he's used from the beginning of the world.

Why hasn't he changed them? Because in almost all cases, *they still work.*

These weapons are three despicable and underhanded entities. They require no introduction because you are already familiar with their work. They claim to be friends of yours but don't believe a word they say. They have been with you at some of the worst moments in your life and surprisingly, nearby during some of the best. You may not recognize their schemes—but that's about to change.

Say, "Hello" to *Doubt, Fear, and Regret.*

DOUBT   FEAR   REGRET

They may appear harmless, but in truth they aim to derail your God-given quest through any means they can. We will meet each one up close and personal—but first, let me describe their tactic. Have you ever known someone who appeared to look out for your best interest, yet had been stabbing you in the back the entire time?

Think of Doubt, Fear, and Regret like those people.

Unfortunately, these nasty influences take up residence in your mind. The more comfortable you are with them, the more difficult it is to get rid of them.

As you begin to follow your quest, they will figuratively come up beside you. They appeal to you, putting their arm around you. They whisper gentle cautions to your sense of self-preservation and speak in a "best friend" tone. They offer tender words such as, "You're taking such a big leap here. *Are you sure about this?* I don't want to see you mess up or get hurt."

It sounds kind. It sounds caring. You begin to wonder if they're right. It certainly *feels* right. You begin to ponder their "words of encouragement." After all, they're only thinking about what's best for you (sarcasm implied).

Do those voices ring a bell?

Let's explore *modus operandi* to find out if they are friend or foe.

DOUBT

The first "friend" to show up is typically *Doubt*. He appears most often in the space where you seek to DISCERN God's call. He's the skeptic of the three. He questions and criticizes every action—cultivating uncertainty in your life. Doubt finds it hard to believe anything, especially if you believe what you've heard is really from God. Doubt "counsels" asking, "Are you sure it is God speaking to you? Why would God want to speak to *you*? Everyone will think you are crazy if you say, 'God told me this' or 'God told me that.'"

But here's the thing: Doubt is not just a voice you hear within you. He sneaks into discussions you have with others. When you hear criticism or harsh questions which stir up confusion, you know he's nearby.

I'm not talking about healthy accountability or genuine curiosity issues from those who seek to provide wise counsel in your life. That's healthy; that's good! Wise counsel may challenge you, but the goal of such questions is clarity, not confusion.

Doubt, on the other hand, loves confusion.

Why? Because confusion leads to indecision. Indecision puts the brakes on your desire to respond to God's call. Doubt's mission is to stop you before you even get started. The confusing voice of Doubt is the enemy to the clear voice of God.

If Doubt is not successful in stalling your intent to move forward, he has friends to finish the job. Think of it as tag-team wrestling. If one can't get you, the other steps in. Their combined goal is the wrecking of your response to God's call. If Doubt has a difficult time creating the necessary confusion, he looks to Fear to enter the ring.

FEAR

Fear is less subtle. He's an alarmist. A *loud* alarmist. He shouts about every little thing which could go wrong if you listen to God and actually embrace the *DARE*. Fear shakes you awake from a deep slumber. He puts you in panic mode, dumping a myriad of disastrous scenarios into your mind.

Where Doubt is the confusion creator; Fear is the anxiety agitator.

Fear causes a heart to race and the imagination to go haywire. He wants you to run away as fast as possible from the faith-action God is calling you to take.

Fear has the ability to show up in areas beyond inner thoughts. Fear hides his presence within the words of people who are closest to you. When you hear someone say, "I love you and I don't want to see you hurt," be aware. Fear could be in the room. Again, this takes discernment. That is why *DISCERN* is the first step of your Quest Compass. You need to lean into wise counsel. I'm not being critical of those who love you. Of course, they want the best for you. However, at times the people who love you the most react out of their own sense of self-preservation versus directing you toward the leading of God's voice or the God-picture you see.

If Doubt can't deter you and Fear can't forestall your momentum, they will call in their reliable partner in crime, *Regret*. They figure if Regret can't get you to quit, nothing can.

REGRET

Regret is a roughshod reminder of the past. He digs up missed opportunities or blemished moments to throw in your face. He seeks to shut you down once and for all—no matter how vicious his assault must be. Regret defends his stance—stating if you've failed before, you will fail again. He continues his barrage with all the reasons why he is right—digging up "proof" to back his claim. He figures if you focus on the times you've come up short in the past, you won't bother to try again.

Regret is dauntless.

He brings up evidence as far back as childhood. He reminds you what teachers have pronounced over you. He flashes hurtful words spoken in the past—recreating its sting in the present. He surfaces past sins long-forgiven. He wants you to believe you aren't worthy to hear from God. His claims on your worth shift to conclude you aren't up to the challenge of fulfilling God's call. "And by the way," he continues, "here is a list of every possible reason why."

Hear me when I say this to you:

Doubt, Fear, and Regret are liars!

They will do whatever they can to stop God's work in you and through you. *BUT*, they have absolutely no power over you unless you give it to them. These voices maintain their power when you give them an ear. They require a listening head and heart in order for you to heed the venom they speak. But, you have the power to overcome. Though they are voices every person wrestles with—they do not have a chance to survive if you reject their lies.

The truth is Doubt, Fear, and Regret are terrified of you. They know exactly whose you are and whose authority you carry. They know God is your Daddy. They know you are a child of the King. They tremble at the thought of you fulfilling your quest—which is why they are relentless and desperate in their work against you.

BIG IDEA

The truth is Doubt, Fear, and Regret are terrified of you. They know exactly whose you are and whose authority you carry.

The Bible says:

You, dear children, are from God and have overcome them, because the One who is in you is greater than the one who is in the world.

- 1 John 4:4 NIV

That is GREAT news!

But, here is where the plot thickens:

Doubt, Fear, and Regret are only gatekeepers to a far more subversive and underhanded group of agents. We will deal with them in the next chapter. For now, just keep in mind that Doubt, Fear, and Regret may be fierce opponents—but they are stoppable. They become weakened once you recognize them.

How do you identify them?

You learn to recognize *how* they operate. Then you *reject* their claims. It's not easy, but through a commitment to the Word, prayer, and wise counsel—they can be turned away.

The fight is on. You have what it takes to learn how to fight—and win.

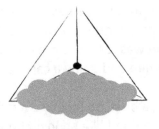

CHAPTER 17:
COMFORT, CREDIBILITY,
AND CONTROL

Recently, I was walking through FutureWorld in EPCOT on a particularly rainy day. This wasn't a typical "Florida 3 o'clock flash-storm" kind of day. It was a "hunker down and grab the rain gear" day. Through a sea of Mickey ponchos, I noticed a young boy standing with his parents. He must have been 7 or 8, so he wasn't little per se. There were two things about him which caught my attention.

First, he didn't seem to care about the rain. While his parents stood beneath a nearby overhang, avoiding the sheets of falling precipitation, he chose to let the full force of it fall on him. It was as if the downpour enhanced the fun. The second thing was his intense dance moves as the rain fell. He bounced in sync with the atmospheric music which permeated the area. He bobbed his head, eyes closed. He sprang forward and back, then shimmied side-to-side. His arms soared through the air in karate-like chops as he spun around.

He didn't notice or care what others thought. He didn't have time for that. He moved—totally engaged with the music—without a single hesitation or inhibition. His parents didn't try to reel him in or settle him down. They loved it. He was lost in another world. I was rather tempted to join him and enjoy a carefree moment too.

Without missing a beat, he looked over at me. He smiled in a way which seemed like an invitation to jump in and join the fun of his one-man dance party. I almost did.

But I was suddenly cut short. I heard a voice inside my head utter a single, condescending statement: *You're an adult.*

I shrank back in the moment. Instead, I simply smiled at the boy's parents, gave the boy a glance of admiration, and continued on my walk in the rain.

It took me less than a minute to realize I had missed out. A single, critical thought had stolen my courage for something fun and adventurous. I looked behind me in the direction of the family, but they had disappeared into the Florida downpour. The opportunity had passed.

Oh to be a kid again, right?

––––––––––

As kids, we weren't afraid to jeopardize life and limb for the sake of adventure. We didn't care what other people thought. We didn't have a reputation to protect or an internal need to ask if it was okay to try. We simply followed our hearts. As we got closer to middle school, something began to change; we were introduced to the whispers of Doubt, Fear, and Regret. We began to hear them in the teasing barbs of peers or in the over-protective warnings of our parents. These internal judges—Doubt, Fear, and Regret—demanded we heed them in order to be liked, fit in, and make the grade.

By the time we entered our teen years we had already begun making room in our young lives for what I term the three desires of life: Comfort, Credibility, and Control. Once they set up house in our young adult minds, they were there for good. Eviction would be next to impossible.

Now that they are firmly rooted in our lives, these three desires will do anything to lead us away from embracing our *DARE* and facing the challenge. Doubt, Fear, and Regret are only puppets; Comfort, Credibility, and Control are the puppet masters.

Comfort

Comfort is a preoccupation with obtaining and keeping anything which makes us feel safe, secure, and satisfied.

For example, our incomes provide for safety, security, and satisfaction. That's a good thing. It allows us to put food on the table and have a roof over our heads. If we are wise with our budgets, we may even be able to buy some nice things.

Over time, we become comfortable with what we have. After all, we've earned it.

But God's call can present the challenge of having to choose between maintaining our current standard of living or being obedient. The *DARE* threatens our comfort zone, something we may have worked very hard to obtain and keep.

It's not easy, is it? You won't find any judgement here. Such a scenario or something like it happens to every one of us at one time or another, more than we care to admit. We all like to be comfortable.

But Scripture has shown us that God does not work within our comfort zones. He always draws us beyond its borders in order for us to learn to trust Him more.

When God presents a *DARE*, it is likely you will be asked to sacrifice an element of Comfort. God's call may require you to pick up and move to a different city, give up a job that you love, or cut out some expenses you've come to enjoy. It could also be as simple as engaging in an inconvenient conversation you didn't plan on having, and now you might miss the start time of the movie you were out to see. Whatever the size or scope of His call—the leading will likely irritate or even infuriate your Comfort.

You'll know the moment Comfort shifts into defense mode. Maybe it shows up in you as a sigh or a frown.

Maybe it's an off-handed comment or criticism which creeps out under your breath. Whatever it may look or sound like, be aware Comfort has realized—even before you have—that God is encroaching upon its territory.

Credibility

Credibility is obsessed with what others think about us. It motivates us to work our proverbial rear ends off in order to impress others and earn respect for our achievements. We love it when others acknowledge us or celebrate something we've done. It feels great. It feeds something within. Social media, and more specifically the addictions surrounding it, proves this inner drive for credibility to be an overwhelmingly true obsession.

Credibility can find its identity in a variety of sources. It could be the position we hold at work or the title bestowed on us through an organization. It doesn't have to be something big either. Credibility may work its influence into things as simple as how we want to look if we ran into someone at the gym or in the Sunday worship service. Our human nature clings to a compulsion to perform, to look good, and to put our best foot forward.

When God calls you to a *DARE*, the Credibility alarms inevitably sound off. They cause you to consider an array of imaginary scenarios, where each one plays out the reaction from others if you were to follow through on what God has told you.

Credibility whispers from the shadows:

"They will they lose respect for you."

"They will think you're crazy."

"They will talk behind your back."

Credibility delegates Doubt, Fear, and Regret to wreak havoc in your thinking. It wants you to panic at the thought of being disrespected or worse yet, being rejected for following through with God's direction.

Control

The last and most dangerous of our three desires is Control.

It knows exactly what it wants. It steers our thoughts and actions to obtain it. Control wants scenarios, situations, and circumstances to unfold exactly how it has envisioned them down to exact details. It feels threatened every time something changes. Control makes plans such as, "By the time I'm 40, I'll be married with two daughters, have a six-figure income, and live in San Diego."

I smile when I hear an aspirational, young person forecast something like that. I smile and consider my own moments in which I thought I had it all planned out. I look at them and think to myself, "Aren't they cute?"

The problem is Control isn't cute. It's a tyrant. It can get frustrated, angry, and spiteful in a moment's notice. If things don't go as planned, it can propel us into a nasty fight. The worst version of ourselves comes out in times when the picture in our mind is threatened by the challenges of the present.

Ironically, God often works in situations which prove to be a deep challenge for us. This doesn't mean God orchestrates pain or suffering to "challenge us." God is a loving Daddy. He doesn't "throw" a challenge our way in order to test our allegiances to serve His "ego." What He does, however, is change us through the resistance we experience so we become more like Him. And when this starts to happen—our Control is the first to be threatened.

When God calls you, beckoning you through an actionable *DARE*, Control is quick to throw a tantrum. This outrage may not be visible to others. It reveals its presence as it draws instant battle lines in your mind. If Control can't draw you toward panic, it will move to convince you with slick reasoning. It can be sneaky. It can sound "safe." It may even seem reasonable at the time. But if you listen to its intent—deep down it demands its agenda, its way. It wants to avoid God "messing things up" for you.

Comfort, Credibility, and Control are incredibly subversive. They don't come into the light or admit their identity or schemes. That's why they send Doubt, Fear, and Regret in to do their dirty work. They know in the light, their ugly motives are fully exposed.

The truth is Doubt, Fear, and Regret are slick sentiments who serve one thing and one thing only—Pride. **BIG IDEA**

151

Selfish pride was the exact tool the Enemy used to deceive and shatter Adam and Eve from being the reflective mirrors of God's goodness on the earth. If you are to embrace God's call and reflect His glory—a fork in the road waits for you. To be obedient to the call, you must face the challenge of your quest head on. This requires you to accept the *DARE* and put your Comfort, Credibility, and Control into God's hands.

God is your true Comfort. He is your provision and protection. Everything else is temporal and could be gone tomorrow.

God is your true source for Credibility. Not one single individual alive has the ability to know you the way He does. All that matters is what He thinks and says about you. The rest is simply opinion.

God is the one truly in Control. Any effort of your own to take Control will only complicate matters and steer your quest off course. God's leading is better than your own limited insight. He is worthy of your trust and will take you to the places He deems as good.

The sooner you recognize that your Comfort, Credibility, and Control are trying to manipulate your quest, the sooner you can turn them over to God and keep pressing forward. In the next chapter, I'll show you three dead giveaways which will allow you to shine a light on their activities and then watch them scatter like Florida cockroaches.

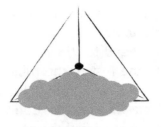

CHAPTER 18:
EXCUSES, EXAGGERATIONS, AND EXIT STRATEGIES

How do you really know when Comfort, Credibility, and Control are trying to manipulate you?

Our internal battles can be misleading, making it hard to remain objective. But there is a way you can illuminate their involvement and call them out. Fortunately for us, an event in Scripture reveals their tactics. This historical account exposes the motives of the forces which work fiercely against you.

In the book of Numbers, we find the account of Moses. He had sent twelve Hebrew spies into the Promised Land to learn firsthand what it was like. This was the land God had promised His followers to be their home hundreds of years earlier. That promise laid in the cusp of fulfillment. It was about to be a moment of great celebration of a long-awaited gift come to fruition.

Of course, Moses already believed what God had told him about the land and how it flowed with milk and honey (meaning it was a land of great abundance and joy). Yet, it was important to Moses for these chosen spies to see it firsthand for themselves and bring back a good report to the rest of the tribes. After 40 days, these twelve men returned from their expedition. They discovered the land was exactly as God said it was. It was so luscious they returned with proof of the abundance as two men carried a single cluster of grapes on a pole between them because it was *that large*. Now that's abundance!

Let's see what happened as these men report all they saw in the land:

They came back to Moses and Aaron and the whole Israelite community at Kadesh in the Desert of Paran. There they reported to them and to the whole assembly and showed them the fruit of the land. They gave Moses this account:

"We went into the land to which you sent us, and it does flow with milk and honey! Here is its fruit. But the people who live there are powerful, and the cities are fortified and very large. We even saw descendants of Anak there. The Amalekites live in the Negev; the Hittites, Jebusites and Amorites live in the hill country; and the Canaanites live near the sea and along the Jordan."

- Numbers 13:26-29 NIV

Their report matches the promise. The land was just as God said it would be. This should have settled it, right?

From here, they could have simply embraced the *DARE* and moved forward to take possession of the land.

That isn't what happened.

One word in their account changed everything. If you read it again, you'll find the story killer—the word, "but." The entire conversation unraveled when they uttered it.

I have a good friend who playfully defines the word "but" as having originated from the Greek word which means "forget everything I just said."

Think about it the next time you say it.

As soon as the spies uttered the catastrophic word, Caleb—who was on the mission with the other eleven—chose to deal with its detrimental effect. He was unafraid to confront the big "but" which derailed what should have been an exciting and adventurous report.

Then Caleb silenced the people before Moses and said, "We should go up and take possession of the land, for we can certainly do it." But the men who had gone up with him said, "We can't attack those people; they are stronger than we are."

- Numbers 13:30,31a NIV

Read that last line one more time. A sure symptom that Comfort, Credibility, or Control are going to put up a fight is when we begin inventing EXCUSES as to why we shouldn't embrace the *DARE*.

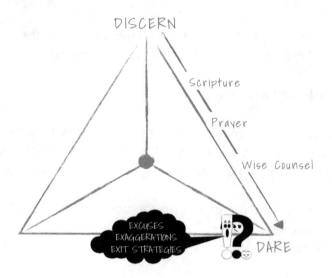

DISCERN

Scripture

Prayer

Wise Counsel

EXCUSES
EXAGGERATIONS
EXIT STRATEGIES

DARE

EXCUSES

When we face a *DARE*, we can become incredibly creative with Excuses on why we shouldn't move forward. We say things and claim we are too old, too young, too busy, too ill-equipped, too insecure, too poor, or too_____ (you fill in the blank). Excuses are the first line of defense to avoid any unpleasantries God invites us to move through.

Caleb, however, was undaunted by such a foe.

He was willing to embrace the *DARE* and face the challenge. He lived in reality. He knew there were giants in the land, but God had promised He would give the territory to the Israelites—giants or no giants. Caleb was certain of God's promise. He was willing to trust God and face the obstacles ahead. To him, moving forward wasn't dangerous; it was a step towards the promise being fulfilled. He knew he had to step up and say something. He sought to rally the "buts" in the group. Unfortunately, his words fell on deaf ears.

And they spread among the Israelites a bad report about the land they had explored. They said, "The land we explored devours those living in it. All the people we saw there are of great size. We saw the Nephilim there (the descendants of Anak come from the Nephilim). We seemed like grasshoppers in our own eyes, and we looked the same to them."

- Numbers 13:31b-33 NIV

Read the last line again. If Excuses aren't enough, Comfort, Credibility, and Control invent *EXAGGERATIONS* to freeze you in your tracks. Doubt, Fear, and Regret seek to paralyze any desire you have to embrace the *DARE*.

EXAGGERATIONS

I don't know about you. But in my world, Exaggerations show up around 3 or 4 a.m. For some reason, the mind runs free and can invent some crazy, CRAZY things about all of the situations which could be working against me. My imagination lists everything that could go wrong if I were to act on faith.

Our own thoughts lie to us and blow everything out of proportion—*way out of proportion.*

Exaggerations are a telling sign that Comfort, Credibility, and Control want to blind you to the call God has set before you.

But if Excuses and Exaggerations don't derail you, they have one last strategy up their sleeves. We can see this third attempt in the continuation of the account.

That night all the members of the community raised their voices and wept aloud. All the Israelites grumbled against Moses and Aaron, and the whole assembly said to them, "If only we had died in Egypt! Or in this wilderness! Why is the Lord bringing us to this land only to let us fall by the sword? Our wives and children will be taken as plunder. Wouldn't it be better for us to go back to Egypt?" And they said to each other, "We should choose a leader and go back to Egypt."

- Numbers 14:1-4 NIV

Read the last line again. When everything goes into panic mode, it's incredibly easy to start formulating *EXIT STRATEGIES.*

EXIT STRATEGIES

Everyone, at one time or another, creates Exit Strategies in case things don't go as planned. Having a Plan B can measure up to having a security blanket.

This doesn't mean healthy preparation isn't wise. Often we need to understand the complexities of situations around us, but not to the point of avoiding obedience to God. If your plan includes an escape plan—a way to run away from God's call—it is a telling sign an Exit Strategy is in play.

These plans create, "Analysis Paralysis." Rather than trusting God, we vacillate back and forth between decisions. We evaluate and re-evaluate, invent, and revise our strategy. In doing so, we cling to a secret hope we will never have to act upon anything. We create multiple plans and feel good about it. In reality, however, we haven't done a thing other than serve our disobedience.

Analysis Paralysis keeps us locked up, protecting the options of staying where we are or going back to where we were. But we certainly are not moving forward.

The Israelites knew this paralysis well. They were wildly afraid of the *DARE* to move forward into God's promises to the point they were willing to get rid of Moses (their connection to God) and go back to slavery in Egypt (from which God has rescued them). *How crazy is that?*

This is how devious Comfort, Credibility, and Control can be. They want you to remove healthy guidance, wise voices, and God's leadership—all for the sake of personal "security."

> There's no way around it. A faith-action will always be a part of God's leading.

BIG IDEA

As you learn to recognize the call from God, you must expect a *DARE* to be part of it. There is no way around it. A faith-action will always be part of God's leading. Doubt, Fear, and Regret will be unleashed to interrupt and dominate the conversation between you and God.

How do we stop them? The moment you hear yourself create an Excuse, Exaggeration, or Exit Strategy, you know the Enemy is working hard against you. Be prepared. His voice speaks in a soothing tone which sounds caring and concerned.

Make no mistake, he is simply appealing to your Comfort, Credibility, and Control. He seeks to use them against you to impeded your obedience. As you grow to recognize these voices, you will have the power to expose such deception every single time. It takes courage, but I promise you it's available to you when you need it.

Ask God for the courage to follow Him. He will give it to you as needed. It will still be up to you to keep moving forward. To do that, I'll give you four principles which will help you push Doubt, Fear, and Regret aside.

But I don't blame you if you want to stop and catch your breath for now.

CHAPTER 19:
HOW TO TRUST

Jean François Gravelet is not a name many would recognize, but he was quite famous in the mid-1800's. Gravelet took the stage name "Charles Blondin" and became known as "The Amazing Blondin."

A natural acrobat from childhood, Jean grew up beneath the circus tents of Europe. When he was 35 years old, he traveled to the United States. In 1859, he found fame for being the first person to cross Niagara Falls on a tightrope. At first, most people believed his claim to be a hoax when he announced his plan to attempt it. They were shocked to find out his claim was true.

Blondin made several crossings. Each time, he introduced new variations:

- He crossed on stilts.
- He crossed in a gorilla suit.
- He crossed with his manager on his back.

- He cooked breakfast for himself halfway through his crossing.
- He pushed a wheelbarrow across.

One time, he asked the crowds if they thought he could push a wheelbarrow across *blindfolded*. They cheered with delight as he traversed the chasm with ease despite his inability to see. He called back to the crowd, asking if they believed he could repeat the trek with the wheelbarrow piled high with potatoes. They roared with accolades as he ventured across without losing a single potato.

Finally, he asked the crowd if they believed he could carry a person across the falls in the wheelbarrow. They screamed their affirmation. Then he asked for a volunteer to get in the wheelbarrow. The crowd laughed and then grew uncomfortably silent when they realized Blondin was serious.

Out of the hushed crowd emerged an older woman. She agreed to go with him across the falls. Blondin helped her into the wheelbarrow and proceeded to carry her across the falls and back again. The crowd was spellbound, in awe of the old woman's willingness to put her life into Blondin's hands.

What they didn't know was she was Blondin's mother.

Accepting a *DARE* from God can be a very scary thing. Often, we feel every ounce of our flesh resisting the *DARE*. Yet, something deeper in our hearts affirms this is the right thing to do.

The call of God puts our belief to the test when we are called to match action to the DARE.

Trust is the challenge which connects belief to action. Charles Blondin's mother not only believed in her son, she trusted him without reservation. We know this because she acted in accordance to her belief. God calls us to do the same thing. We can talk-and-talk-and-talk about belief in God but we must be willing to put such belief into action. When we trust Him without reservation, the adventure we are created for becomes reality.

Whenever I think about The Amazing Blondin and his mother, I see a picture of the kind of faith God longs for us to experience.

Imagine for a moment that Jesus is The Amazing Blondin and you are the one in the wheelbarrow. There's a lot happening in such a trek, but there are four simple things to help you make it across.

First, imagine yourself on the tightrope with Him. A myriad of questions would scream for your attention. "Is it tight enough? Will it hold your weight? Will the blowing wind affect it?" You just don't know. You have to accept the tension of the rope is what it should be.

In the same way, you have to get comfortable with mystery. God doesn't always give you the answers you think you need. He often says, "You just have to trust Me in this." We may not like it, but we must accept He has the details under control and move forward. That is what makes it faith.

Second, imagine yourself in the wheelbarrow again. I can pretty much assume you won't be moving around much. The wind is blowing. The rope is moving up and down. You will likely still yourself in the wheelbarrow as He carries you across.

In the same way, you need to rest in the Word of God. His Word provides you something solid to hold onto when you follow God into the unfamiliar. Everything around may seem to change its perspective, but you can rest assured the Bible will always give you what you need.

Third, imagine what it must have been like for Blondin's mother as she journeyed across the falls. Do you think her son spoke to her as they spanned the roaring chasm? I'm certain he did. There's no record of their conversation, but I'm sure he assured her every step of the way.

"I have you, Mom."

"It won't be long now, Mom."

"You can relax, Mom."

"I've got everything under control."

In the same way you need to be listening for the voice of Jesus as He carries you into the challenges of your quest. There will be temptations through the journey. You may be tempted to panic. Jesus promises to be the voice behind you, showing you the way to go (Isaiah 30:21). He will encourage and remind you He is *always* with you.

Don't worry, I have you.
It won't be long now.
You can relax.
I've got everything under control.
Thank you for trusting me.

As you respond to God's call and embrace the *DARE*, Jesus will be with you every step of the way. There is no reason for Doubt, Fear, or Regret to plague your journey. They have no power over Jesus and, if you don't give it to them, they have no power over you.

Lastly, remember as you face your challenge, to focus on the other side. I've learned one of the secrets of tightrope walkers is to not look down. They keep their eyes focused ahead. At times, when the rope sways or their balance is put to the test, the best way to recover is to fix their sight on the other side.

In the same way, you must look to the promises of God. It is easy to become paralyzed when you feel like situations around you are out of control. You can quickly lose your "spiritual" balance.

Doubt will remind you how thin the rope looks.
Fear demands you look down.
Regret wants you to look backwards.

Don't listen to their lies.

God promises He will never abandon you. He will get you to where He is taking you if you trust Him and act on His leading. Focus on the other side. Set your eyes on the promises of God.

How do you actionally embrace the *DARE* and face the challenges of your quest?

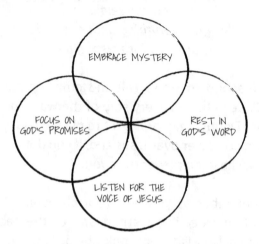

Get comfortable with mystery.
Rest in the Word of God.
Listen for the voice of Jesus.
Look to the promises of God.

These four principles may seem deceptively simple, but you and I know each one of them takes a lifetime to learn. The discipline of assimilating them into our lives is part of the adventure. Every day you live inside the adventure, you grow, learn, and become the person God designed you to be. You are free to do more-and-more of what God has created you to do.

Embracing the *DARE* is hard. There's no way around it. There's no shortcut. To live the life beyond imagination that God has uniquely designed you for, you must be willing to take on the challenge of staying the course.

In the world of storytelling, when the hero embraces the *DARE* and faces the challenge, we call this scene "the moment of truth." Those words could not be more accurate when it comes to following God into your quest.

> To live the life beyond imagination that God has uniquely designed you for, you must be willing to take on the challenge of staying the course. **BIG IDEA**

When you accept the *DARE* and face the challenge, it will be your moment of truth. It's the scene which changes you in the deepest places and strengthens your trust into an even closer relationship with the One who created you.

All the while, Heaven applauds and cheers with delight.

Section Five

FOLLOW JESUS COURAGEOUSLY

Isn't it obvious that God-talk without God-acts is outrageous nonsense? James 2:17 MSG

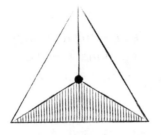

CHAPTER 20:
MAKE IT HAPPEN

The very moment you separate body and spirit, you end up with a corpse. Separate faith and works and you get the same thing: a corpse.

- James 2:26 MSG

The way to get started is to quit talking and begin doing.

- Walt Disney

"Make it happen."

I count myself fortunate to have enjoyed innumerable conversations with Cast Members. As I have observed their daily adventures from working in the parks, I have come to recognize a common theme in 99% of them. Regardless of the season, time of day, weather condition, high attendance, grumpy guests, Cast Members who called in sick that day, or any other of the countless variables which impact the "magic" of Disney,

Cast Members hear one single directive more than any other: "Make it happen."

To some, this objective might sound a bit callous, a compassionless command. However, when it is communicated correctly, it actually provides freedom for creative action.

"Make it happen" is the trump card for self-initiated problem solving, unique work-arounds, and a license to find a new way. It eliminates the wasted time of pointless discussion and debate. Instead, it ignites a thinking process which offers the possibility of a quick resolution.

Cast Members told to "Make it happen" are released to make decisions which benefit their guests, their fellow Cast Members and ultimately The Walt Disney Company. The freedom within "Make it happen" is the number one reason why The Walt Disney Parks and Resorts consistently score high in guest satisfaction and receive repeat business.

But "Make it happen" goes beyond Disney. When we look close, we see how Walt wasn't the originator of such a freeing concept.

Let's think about a "Make it happen" directive in the context of The Quest Compass. As we move from the DARE corner of The Quest Compass, we discover the heart of the challenge. This may not seem like rocket science but the next step in your journey is to simply DO what God is asking of you.

You and I know how embracing a *DARE* will lead to facing a challenge which will always prove to be difficult. But there is no way around it. A faith-action is not complete until we *act*. We can talk about it. We can brainstorm. We can worry about it. We can avoid it. We can sit on our hands and ponder the challenge. But none of these are actionable. None of these are obedience. None of these are actually following the quest Jesus has put before us. It's simply stalling.

We cannot call it faith just because we talk about it. The hard truth about being a disciple of Jesus is the fact we must move past talk. Faith isn't faith until it becomes action.

This is why most people get stuck between the *DARE* and the *DO*. I have been stuck in this spot many times. You'll find yourself in this limbo at various points too, if you aren't there now.

Pushing through this no-man's land and following the quest God created you for is where your relationship with Him becomes the most visible to others. It is the challenge which produces the greatest change in and around you. But you should never deny the fact that you get stuck from time to time. Everyone does.

But you *can* move beyond it!

When you know what God has told you and the faith-action required to move forward, Fear releases Excuses, Exaggerations, and Exit Strategies right on cue. We are tempted to stop and reconsider the next step. But just like standing in wet cement, the longer one contemplates moving forward the less likely it will be possible to move at all.

The longer we take to *DO* the *DARE*, the more likely the *DARE* won't get done.

Unfortunately, there is another problem which I have found to plague me when I grow uncomfortable with the challenge.

I can be tempted to turn away from the *DARE* and return to *DISCERN*. If I am not comfortable with what God is asking, I might stall and reason the ways I must've heard Him incorrectly. The whispers of Doubt are simply asking me to reconsider, to be certain.

I think to myself, "Perhaps I should go back and wait until I hear something different or God changes His mind."

I can promise you, such a mindset can keep us waiting an enormously long time. God doesn't change His mind.

Though I may have learned to yield quicker and embrace the *DARE* more often, it is fair to say that the inner work-arounds we can get caught up in are always in play. The struggle is always there because 98% of the time the journey through the challenge is a mental battle.

Think back to a time you had to do something which scared the living daylights out of you. Maybe it was your first jump from a high dive, the first time you asked a girl to dance, your first major job interview, or even your first-time skydiving. If you put yourself in the shoes of your younger self, you are likely to remember the nervousness and fear leading up to a moment of action.

But when you actually acted in the moment, didn't it feel as if you were on auto-pilot? Perhaps it even felt surreal or like an out-of-body experience. That's because you had already won the mental battle. Taking action was easier than you thought because you mentally worked through it. You were able to see the action through, even if you belly flopped on the water, the girl turned you down, the employer went a different direction, or...well, since you're reading this, the skydiving attempt must've turned out okay. While it may have been incredibly difficult leading up to taking action, *actually doing it* was pretty much a snap.

The struggle is always there because 98% of the time the journey through any challenge is a mental battle. **BIG IDEA**

I recently sat with a member of our church who was wrestling with a decision that needed to be made. Using The Quest Compass, together we sought to help determine what God was saying to him and what action he should take. This young man was quite an intelligent and spiritually aware individual. He was stalling the course of our discussion for one reason—he knew what God was telling him to do would be a definite challenge to his Credibility. I affirmed his reasoning and why he wrestled so hard with it. I didn't seek to hide the reality of the challenge—but I did want to help him face it. We talked for a while and I asked him how he planned to move forward. He hemmed and hawed for over an hour. He circled, essentially landing on a plan to wait for some kind of confirmation. He fed me Excuses, Exaggerations, and an Exit Strategy or two.

Keep in mind God had already spoken to this young man. I was certain God had been extremely clear about the call He had given. It matched everything I knew of God's character, His Word, and His ways. As he kept discussing alternative plans, I suggested that if he needed confirmation, he should go ahead and face the challenge. I was confident he would find God's leading when he needed it. In my mind, there is no better way to learn than to *just do* what you believe God has said to do. This young man shook his head with great frustration at my counsel and said, "Steven, I just wanted you to support me."

I was taken aback slightly. I didn't understand the gap between us. In truth, I actually had been supporting him. Our hour-long conversation had been filled with me imparting belief and affirming a courage and confidence to proceed into what God had said. But this was not what he had been looking for. He just wanted someone to agree with him—someone to help him avoid the challenge which he had felt was intimidating and impossible in his mind.

The truth is: we can drag our feet, seek out a thousand more confirmations, and wholeheartedly hope God will change His mind. None of it will work. When God lays out a *DARE* leading into a challenge, the best thing we can do is "Make it happen." God does not forget a *DARE*. You cannot proceed in His call on your life without embracing a step He puts before you.

Moving from the *DARE* to the *DO* leads us through uncharted territory. Though the unknown is scary, but it is where the adventure happens. We don't know the end result. We aren't given the final puzzle piece ahead of time. God knows the outcome even when we don't. This is what makes our quests amazing. In the midst of the challenge, God follows through on what He promises to do. He has to. We can't do it without Him.

"Don't be afraid, I've redeemed you. I've called your name. You're Mine. When you're in over your head, I'll be there with you. When you're in rough waters, you will not go down. When you're between a rock and a hard place, it won't be a dead end—Because I am God, your personal God, The Holy of Israel, your Savior."

- Isaiah 43:2 MSG

With a heart and mind full of the knowledge of God's promises, you can find courage to *DO* whatever He asks you to. No matter how great the *DARE* or the fear which rises up, you can do this because God is with you. And if God is with you, who or what can stand in your way?

I understand if you think I've painted an unrealistic strategy with a "Make it happen" mindset. I admit it looks much better on paper than it does in the reality of our everyday world. But I promise there is freedom for creativity, initiative, and meaningful impact inside of it.

In the next few chapters, I will provide you with three steps (Plan, Partner and Point of no return) to help you be best equipped to "Make it happen" in the real world. My desire is for you to be able to move through the challenge of your quest with more courage than you've ever known. I won't water down the *DARE*, nor soften the challenge you are called to pass through. I have no desire to cheat you out of the joy of following Jesus wholeheartedly, even if it means embracing the hard parts. This section is designed to provide you with all the momentum you need to slice through the mental battle, face the challenge, and keep moving forward.

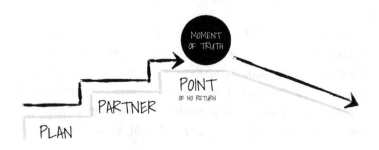

Remember, the best part of any story, whether it's a movie, a book, or a TV show, is the moment the protagonist chooses to face the challenge. Despite the voices of Doubt, Fear, and Regret, our hero embraces the *DARE*, puts their game face on and chooses to cross the line into the unknown.

The moment of truth has arrived; it's time to *Make it happen.*

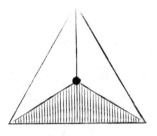

CHAPTER 21:
MAKE A PLAN

Moving from *DARE* to *DO* can be overwhelming. It can feel like standing on the edge of a high cliff which faces a separate cliff ten feet away. In between is a deep chasm. It is impossible to simply step across the gap or place one foot on both sides. In order to reach the other side, you have to run as fast as you can, jump with momentum, and be willing to be airborne across the gap.

The most effective way to face your challenge and begin moving from *DARE* to *DO*, is to quickly make a plan. Don't hesitate. Waiting only allows Doubt, Fear, and Regret to organize against you. The sooner you form a plan, the sooner you can move forward.

Your plan doesn't require any big strategy, multiple steps, or anything else which might complicate your ability to follow through.

Just remember to:

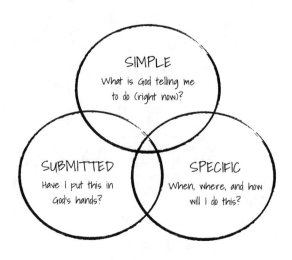

Keep it SIMPLE.
Make it SPECIFIC.
Leave it SUBMITTED to God.

Keep it SIMPLE.

Answer the question, "What is God telling me to do?"

Don't overthink. God is not a god of confusion. He doesn't want you to stumble around, looking at a buffet of options as you grow weary before you even start. Your plan should be short, actionable, and to the point.

For bigger plans, they simply need to be broken into the first simple, actionable step. You can simply answer the question, "What is God asking me to do right now?" You should be able to state this plan in one sentence. Here are some examples:

"God is telling me to reconcile with my friend who I'm not speaking to."

"God is telling me to stand up for a coworker who was wrongly accused."

"God is telling me to apologize to the grocery cashier I was angry with yesterday."

"God is telling me to share my faith-story with my boss."

"God is telling me to turn down the promotion my company has offered me."

"God is telling me to reach out to the weird neighbor across the street."

Are any of these complicated or confusing? I don't think so. You can certainly recognize the *DARE* in every one of them. You can be certain a *DARE* will be included in whatever God is asking of you.

Make it SPECIFIC.

Upon forming a simple statement regarding what God is asking you to *DO*, it's time to respond. At this point, you will probably sense nervous apprehension because you are about to declare the action you will take.

Ask yourself, "When, where, and how will I do this?" By answering these three simple questions, you will have formed your plan. Let's use the previously mentioned statements to see what a plan might look like:

"God is telling me to reconcile with my friend who I'm not speaking to."
                    I will call them at 3:00pm today.

"God is telling me to stand up for my coworker who was wrongly accused."

I'll go to Human Resources tomorrow, before work, to make an appointment.

"God is telling me to apologize to the grocery cashier I got angry with yesterday."

I will go back to store after dinner tonight and ask to speak with her.

"God is telling me to share my faith-story with my boss."

I will invite my boss out to lunch next Tuesday.

"God is telling me to turn down the promotion my company has offered me."

I will send a response email right now.

"God is telling me to reach out to the weird neighbor across the street."

I will go tonight and invite them to dinner at our house.

These examples demonstrate a specific response to whatever God might be asking. When you create a plan, you commit to face the challenge and follow through in obedience to God's call. The plan eliminates variables and scenarios which could impede your quick response.

Remember, when you plan, you step into the actionable, challenge side of The Quest Compass. You will be tempted to abandon your plan and retreat. Be aware that the more time you give yourself to respond will only increase the second-guessing you will be tempted to make.

This is why I encourage and challenge you to plan fast and act quickly. The sooner the better. While there is not a benefit to being hasty or emotion-driven, there is benefit in removing the opportunity for Doubt, Fear, or Regret to edge into a plan which lingers too long.

Leave it SUBMITTED to God.

Once you have made a plan, commit to it and put it in God's hands.

This means—talk with Him about it. Share your plan. Let Him know what action you have committed to. Then, if you are tempted to change it, delay it, or abandon it—you become aware that you are taking the plan out of God's hands. In essence, you are abandoning your co-laboring initiative with Him to allow your Comfort, Credibility, and Control to take over.

Don't do it.

You will be tempted—this is human—but I implore you to keep in step with God. He is with you—leading you into deep relationship with Him. Don't miss out on the adventure. Your quest is off and running, don't let it be detoured. Give your plan to God and let Him hold onto it.

You can face and move through any challenge God leads you into. From the time you make your plan, to the moment you follow through, ask God to fill you with courage to do whatever He is asking. He will provide you all you need to accomplish His will in the course of your challenge. Ask Him to keep you focused on why you are doing this, and not on what might happen or what could go wrong.

We humans are incredibly gifted at creating false scenarios in our heads and inventing outcomes which simply don't exist. Submit your plan to God and leave it with Him. I've learned it is better off in His hands anyway. It's important to note that when you put a plan into God's hands, He does have the right to alter it. He may slow it down or speed it up. But that will be His choice, not yours.

 BIG IDEA — A God-inspired plan that is simple, specific, and completely submitted to Him will carry you over the gap with all the momentum you need to land on the other side.

I remember one time God had made me aware that I had hurt someone in my church with a sarcastic comment. I heard this person was pretty upset. I felt terrible about it and wanted to apologize. I also wondered if I had damaged our friendship beyond repair. It was already getting late into the evening when I became aware of this offense that I had committed. I also happened to be in the middle of Disney's Animal Kingdom.

Right there, I made a plan to call him first thing in the morning and quickly prayed under my breath for God to help me bring a quick resolution to this predicament.

It hadn't been more than five minutes after I made that plan and given it over to God, when I saw the person I had offended in the crowd walking in my direction. I had no idea he was in the park. We chatted pleasantries for a couple of minutes but it was obvious we were both feeling a little awkward. I was certain God had changed the plan. I quickly apologized for what I had said and asked for his forgiveness. He forgave me right there in the moment. Everything changed and our friendship was back on solid ground.

It was amazing to see God take my plans and alter the timeline for the sake of quicker resolution. God knew something about my plan that I didn't. He knew my friend was already in the park, so He pushed up the timeline of my plan and gave me the opportunity to do what needed to be done.

A God-inspired plan that is simple, specific, and completely submitted to Him will carry you over the gap with all the momentum you need to land on the other side.

The best part is that God is already there to catch you no matter how you land.

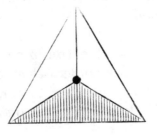

CHAPTER 22:
PARTNER UP

Jesus walked through great challenges in the course of His ministry:

- He faced temptations from Satan in the wilderness.
- He knew rejection from His own family.
- The congregation of His local synagogue attempted to throw Him off a cliff.
- He received constant criticism from the Pharisees—those who should have recognized Him.
- He was betrayed by one of His disciples.

Every day Jesus had to face new and difficult challenges. As the Son of God, He embraced each challenge with perfect love, truth, mercy, and grace. He certainly felt the weight of the challenge—He was human after all—but He was never deterred. His mind was fully aware of the climactic challenge that His ministry moved towards—His impending, torturous death on the cross. It was for this reason He had been sent into the world.

On the night before His crucifixion, Jesus led His disciples outside the city of Jerusalem to the Garden of Gethsemane, His favorite place to pray. He knew the horrors waiting for Him were only hours away.

He took Peter and the two sons of Zebedee along with Him, and He began to be sorrowful and troubled. Then He said to them, "My soul is overwhelmed with sorrow to the point of death. Stay here and keep watch with Me."

- Matthew 26:37,38 NIV

As Jesus prepared to meet the greatest challenge one could ever face, He chose not to be alone. He desired companionship. He needed His friends to be with Him. He saw their company as a source of strength to keep moving forward. As our perfect example, Jesus modeled the need for community, especially within the space and time of His absolute darkest moment.

Since we are created for relationship, it makes sense God doesn't want us to face our challenges alone. Community must be an integral part of pressing forward. When we DISCERN God's call and make a plan to follow through, it is the presence of a trusted friend which keeps us from losing our way, getting distracted, or just giving up.

Every challenge before us will inevitably expose a weakness within us. Why? Because there can be a minefield of opposition between the DARE and the DO.

This is why Jesus sent the disciples out in twos.

Later the Master selected seventy and sent them ahead of Him in pairs to every town and place where He intended to go.

- Luke 10:2 MSG

Jesus called the Twelve to Him, and sent them out in pairs. He gave them authority and power to deal with the evil opposition.

- Mark 6:7 MSG

Even when Jesus sent His disciples to take care of menial tasks, He sent them out by twos.

After saying these things, Jesus headed straight up to Jerusalem. When He got near Bethphage and Bethany at the mountain called Olives, He sent off two of the disciples with instructions: "Go to the village across from you. As soon as you enter, you'll find a colt tethered, one that has never been ridden. Untie it and bring it. If anyone says anything, asks, 'What are you doing?' say, 'His Master needs him.'"

- Luke 19:28-31 MSG

Jesus knew the importance of having someone accompany you through the greatest to the least of challenges.

It's better to have a partner than go it alone. Share the work, share the wealth. And if one falls down, the other helps, but if there's no one to help, tough!

- Ecclesiastes 4:9,10 MSG

With each and every challenge you face in your quest, you need someone to partner with. This individual helps you to keep moving forward until you act. Likewise, you are called to offer the same support and accountability to others. Without a partner, I can tell you from experience, you will rarely follow through.

We are not strong enough, determined enough, or possess the endurance to go it alone. Whatever God sets before any one of us cannot be accomplished in an isolated vacuum. We each need someone to come alongside us for whatever challenge we are going to face. If Jesus needed it—so do we.

 BIG IDEA Since we are created for relationship, it makes sense God doesn't want us to face our challenges alone.

Many people have told me they can pursue a quest on their own, without the need of a friend or someone to stand with them. I've yet to see one follow through. Accountability is key to move from the *DARE* to the *DO*.

But let's also take a moment to discuss accountability.

In the back of my mind, I wonder if so many of us desire to "go it alone" because we fear what accountability could mean. Do we shy away from a beneficial relationship just because we don't understand how to successfully operate inside of one?

The truth is, many within the church have turned the word "accountability" into something it isn't. Holding someone accountable is never paired with an attitude which says, "Gotcha!" when someone fails or screws up.

It's not a system to pile on disappointment or surface failures. Such an attitude or language is vastly unlike Jesus. Unfortunately, most of us have faced such an air at one time or another—thus we slink away from wanting to invite and include others in our quests. We secretly fear they could turn on us if we fail to follow through.

Biblical accountability is more of a support than a sneak attack. It means steadying someone if they stagger and catching them before they fall. At times, this may mean carrying them over the inner hurdles and through the external harassments. If they do happen to fall, accountability doesn't condemn, it picks them back up, dusts them off, treats their scrapes, and nudges them back on the right path again. That is accountability.

How could having a partner make a difference for your challenge?

You already have a simple, specific, and submitted plan for action. It's time to share your plan with someone else. This may be the same person who provided you wise counsel when you were discerning God's call. It might be someone different. Whoever it is, they should be willing to stand with you as you move towards the other side of the challenge.

I have found this is best accomplished by understanding three simple phases within the accountability role:

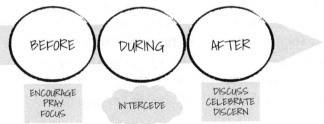

BEFORE
ENCOURAGE
PRAY
FOCUS

DURING
INTERCEDE

AFTER
DISCUSS
CELEBRATE
DISCERN

1. PARTNER BEFORE: When you share your plan (what, when, where, and how), ask this person to call you shortly before you implement your plan.

For example, let's say your plan is to call your friend today at 3:30 to ask for forgiveness. Use the partnership and accountability relationship to share your plan and then ask them, "Could you call me at 3:00 today to encourage me and pray with me?"

How likely would you be to follow through, if a partner contacted you half an hour before you planned to take action? If you answered, "Very likely," you're right.

2. PARTNER DURING: Ask your partner to pray for you as you act upon what you've committed to do. They might not be physically present with you (although they could be), but their prayers are still heard by God—who is always with you. You have a confidence because you know they are talking with God on your behalf at the same time you are taking action.

3. PARTNER AFTER: Ask your partner to check in with you after you've taken action. Set a time which works for both of you. You might say something like, "Can we talk at 4:30 so I can share how it went?"

Alternatively, if you are providing accountability for someone else—initiate with them and say, "I'll call you at 4:30 to see how it went." When you know there is follow-up, it motivates you to make it happen. Knowing someone is waiting on the other side of the *DO*, gives you the courage to follow through. If fear or a natural hindrance got in the way—there is an opportunity to encourage, re-plan, and choose next steps.

Having a partner with you in the midst of your challenge is one of God's greatest resources. When you, a faithful friend, and God work together to accomplish something, it will expand your faith, deepen your friendship, and broaden God's Kingship.

That's what I call a win-win-win.

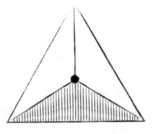

CHAPTER 23:
PASS THE POINT
OF NO RETURN

Between the anticipation of boarding a Disney attraction and the exhilaration of riding a Disney attraction is an emotional zone I call, (cue the echoey voice) "The point of no return." Cast Members call this super-technical location the "loading area."

After you've waited in the queue for a while, you finally reach the room in which the ride vehicle pulls up in front of you. The riders who have just completed their journey unbuckle and unload onto the opposite side of the track. Their squeals of excitement left over from their adventure quickens your pulse. Your turn has come. You know you're next.

The safety gate opens and you step into the ride vehicle. You pull a seatbelt across your body or lower the lap bar until it clicks into place. You are locked and loaded. The familiar Disney voice comes over the sound system, "Please keep your hands and arms inside at all times." You can feel your heart pounding in your chest. Suddenly, the vehicle brakes release and you move forward.

You have passed the point of no return.

There's no going back. No matter what happens beyond this point, you cannot get off until the ride comes to a full and complete stop after its journey. Like it or not, you're all in.

As I've mentioned before, 95% of the challenge side of The Quest Compass is a mental battle. It runs almost the full distance between the *DARE* and the *DO*. You have the plan. You have a partner. You have positioned yourself to follow through. Now comes the moment when you just have to *DO* it.

For someone in financial debt who believes God is asking them to make a responsible change in their spending habits, the point of no return could be cutting up their credit cards or selling the car which has outrageous payments.

For someone who is working for an unethical company and believes God wants them to leave a toxic environment, the point of no return could be tendering their resignation even though they have no idea what the future holds.

For someone who knows God has told them to seek forgiveness from a friend, the point of no return simply means dialing their phone number. (Caller ID makes every phone call a point of no return.)

Every parent knows what it feels like to pass the point of no return. We have all heard how no one is ever really ready to have a baby. Speaking as a parent, this is true. But we do it anyway. When your wife comes out of the bathroom holding the little test stick and says, "I'm pregnant," you've both passed the point of no return. Congratulations!

I wish I could give "three simple steps" to make the "doing" easier. But the truth is, faith isn't easy. Following Jesus isn't always easy. But that doesn't mean it isn't right. At this point, enacting the *DO* comes down to you. God is not going to push or force you to follow Him. The choice to "Make it happen" is entirely yours.

God is not going to push or force you to follow Him. The choice to "Make it happen" is entirely yours. **BIG IDEA**

When I was 10 or 11 years old, I remember my dad taught me how to swim. He taught me how to hold my breath, how to breathe out, and how to coordinate my arms and feet to move myself forward. I was quite good at it. There was only one problem. I was terrified of deep water. I had no problem swimming as long as both of my feet could touch the bottom of the pool. If I couldn't feel the bottom at any point, I panicked.

My dad knew that if I was to truly enjoy swimming, I needed to become confident in deep water. He explained how swimming in the deep-end was no different from swimming in the shallow, which only came up to my chest. I'm sure he was right but I had no interest in putting his wisdom to the test. I was content to stay in the shallow end of the pool for life. I could simply admire those who jumped off the high-dive located at the other end of the pool.

One day, I walked past the high dive section on the way to my poolside chair. Suddenly from behind me, two hands reached up under my arms, picked me up off the ground, and threw me into the 10' deep end of the pool. I hit the water with a horrific shock. I pushed to the surface to see who had thrown me in. It was my dad. I cried hard. I swam and kicked to the edge with absolute disdain for what my so-called "loving father" had done to me.

As I climbed up the ladder to exit the pool, he smiled and said, "See, it's no different from swimming in shallow water." I didn't care. I stomped off to find my beach blanket and pout.

A couple of days later, our family went to the pool again. I passed by the diving boards and once again, from out of nowhere, the same hands threw me into the deep water. This time when I came to the surface, I was mad. I swam and kicked to the ladder and told my dad to never, ever, EVER do that again.

He had the nerve to just smile at me.

The next several times our family went to the pool, I changed my route of travel from the shallow-end of the pool to my towel. I avoided walking past the deep-end of the pool altogether. I grew paranoid that my dad was always lurking nearby, just waiting to sneak up on me, and cast me into the watery, bottomless pit of the diving zone.

Several weeks passed and so did my keen awareness of my dad's location at the pool. One day, I inadvertently walked past the deep end of the pool. Suddenly, out of the corner of my eye I saw my dad approaching like a tiger about to pounce on its prey. I knew the inevitable was coming. But this time I wasn't going to give him the satisfaction of throwing me in.

I just jumped into the deep-end before he got to me. My dad smiled at me as I came to the surface. This time I was smiling too. He taught me that sometimes you just have to jump.

Since then, I've loved the deep water.

You may hesitate. You may have genuine fears or concerns to overcome. That's okay. God will lead you through each and every one of them. But you can't avoid the *DO*. To experience the awaiting joys of your God-given quest, you simply have to accept the fact that it requires jumping into the deep end.

Trust me, it's worth it.

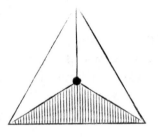

CHAPTER 24:
SOMETHING HAS CHANGED

It's very hard to predict what will happen after you have *DISCERNED* God's call, embraced the *DARE*, faced the challenge, and done what He has asked you to *DO*. You cannot guess the outcome, but you can be certain *something has changed*.

God is delighted when you are willing to set aside your Comfort, Credibility, and Control for His sake. You have authenticated your belief with action. It's one thing to say, "I believe...," but acting on belief is what pleases God most of all.

It's impossible to please God apart from faith. And why? Because anyone who wants to approach God must believe both that He exists and that He cares enough to respond to those who seek Him.

- Hebrews 11:6 MSG

Your faith-action not only puts a huge smile on God's face, but it also releases an answer to one of the requests found in the Lord's Prayer, when Jesus said to His Father, **"...Your Kingdom come, Your will be done, on earth as it is in heaven."**

- Matthew 6:10 NIV

When you move through The Quest Compass, you become a living conduit of God's Kingship. Your faith-actions allow you to be the hands and feet of Jesus to anyone and everyone. It's Jesus' presence and power that does the heavy lifting, so to speak. But it's your trust which allows Him to do it through you.

It's an awesome privilege to work in partnership with the King of the universe. But, it doesn't stop there. Not only does God expand His Kingship in the world through you, He also expands it *within* you.

 BIG IDEA The journey always leaves God's fingerprints behind at the scene. Anything God touches is never the same after.

Your faith-action moves you beyond what has always been familiar and comfortable. That step presents the opportunity for God to now expand those borders.

Every time you face the challenge of doing what God asks of you, He works alongside you. He proves Himself faithful and is with you the entire time. The more you become aware of His steadfast faithfulness, your confidence in Him expands. You gain assurance in territory which was once foreign and unfamiliar. God increases your capacity to trust Him in deeper ways for your next faith-trip around The Quest Compass.

There's a bonus: The journey always leaves God's fingerprints behind at the scene. Anything God touches is never the same after.

The change could be visible immediately.

- Someone responds to the Good News of Jesus being shared with them.
- A person who is ill or injured is miraculously healed.
- A relationship which was broken for years is restored.

I can recount hundreds of stories of how God has changed a person, place, or predicament in a single moment. But those are my stories. I look forward to hearing yours. God's call and invitation happens more and more in your life when you are willing to face your challenges and take the necessary faith-actions.

Witnessing God's immediate and visible influence in any scenario is an amazing thing. It is a privilege when you get to see it in the moment. But know, often His fingerprints are not visible immediately. Like planting seeds in the ground, it may take time to see the fruit God will produce from your faith-actions.

There will also be times when you will take the right faith-action and the result will not go well at all.

Speaking from experience, there have been numerous times when I was absolutely certain I had obeyed God, yet it blew up in my face. Amidst the frustration in the aftermath, I have struggled—questioning if I did the right thing or not. I've caught myself replaying the situation over-and-over in my head, trying to determine where I went wrong. But the more I've experienced these unexpected twists on my own quest, I've come to understand it's simply the Enemy in the form of Regret trying to rob me of the joy of trusting Jesus. Satan wants to deflate my desire to follow the God of my quest. He wants me to rely solely on visible results versus the greater reward of having been drawn closer to Jesus.

Just because we are obedient doesn't mean God will do what we expect Him to do. The outcome is always in His hands. It's not up to us. The difficult element of trust is learning to accept how God works beyond the boundaries of our own expectations.

Is there anyone around who can explain God? Anyone smart enough to tell Him what to do? Anyone who has done Him such a huge favor that God has to ask his advice. Everything comes from Him; everything happens through Him; Everything ends up in Him. Always glory! Always praise! Yes. Yes. Yes.

- Romans 11:33-36 MSG

The only thing which matters is whether we have trusted and obeyed. We are not responsible for the outcome. For better or worse, we can rest in the confidence that God has led us to do the right thing and He is sovereign over the result.

Just because you've been obedient and taken your faith-action, doesn't mean you now get to sit back with a glass of your favorite beverage and tune out. God is up to something and you need to stay aware of His ways and His direction. You certainly don't stop praying. Regardless of the outcome, you need to be observing, listening, and asking God, "What's next?"

His response will inevitably lead you back to the top of The Quest Compass. It will be time to *DISCERN* His voice once again. As you develop your skill with The Quest Compass, you'll begin to notice you may use it several times a day for multiple people and situations. Once you have learned to recognize God's voice, you'll become aware of how often He actually speaks. He's your Daddy. He wants to lead you, encourage you, and even challenge you at times. He'll journey with you around the Compass again because He loves sharing the quest with you.

He's working in you, through you, and with you to change the world. Every time you go around The Quest Compass with Him, it's a new faith adventure and it gets better each time.

I may seem like I'm bringing this journey to a close. Nothing could be further from the truth. You've had the opportunity to learn how to hear God clearly, face any challenge with more courage, and bring about a change as you keep moving forward with confidence. This may seem like enough, but not quite.

There's more.

Section Six

LIGHT YOUR WORLD CONFIDENTLY

Point out the road I must travel; I'm all ears, all eyes before you. - Psalm 143:8b MSG

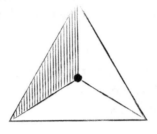

CHAPTER 25:
You Are Here

There is nothing more frustrating for a guest at Walt Disney World than forgetting where they've parked their car. This is especially true at Magic Kingdom or EPCOT parking lots. Both are in the Guinness Book of World Records, tied for fourth on the list of largest parking lots in the world. The EPCOT parking lot alone is over 160 acres, seven million square feet, and the equivalent of 140 football fields. No matter how you look at it—that's a lot of asphalt. If you add the sprawling expanse, the scorching temperatures of July, August, and September, and *then* looking for your car among thousands of others—it will raise a frustration level as high as the thermometer.

This sense of being lost, however, does not come from a lack of information.

The Disney Cast Members who work the parking lots are quite good at informing you where you parked as you board the trams which take you to the front entrance—

sparing you the additional walk. They even encourage you to take a quick photo of the row number in which your car is located, just in case you happen to forget later on.

It's as if they have seen it happen a time or two (or a thousand). This does not mean, however, that I always follow such advice.

Peter Pan 217.

You see, I remember the row number *now*. But when I visited Magic Kingdom a few weeks ago, I completely forgot it as soon as I left my car. You'd think after living almost a decade immersed in the Disney culture, I would've made a note or taken the photo as the Cast Members suggest.

Nope.

I must've been in a hurry, on my phone, or had one of my ADD moments. For whatever reason, I rushed toward the Transportation and Ticket Center and boarded the monorail to Magic Kingdom. Peter Pan 217 was a bygone.

I realized this ominous oversight a few hours later when it came time to return to my car. To add to it, the August Florida weather alerted me to an incoming problem. It was hot and horribly humid and intimated it would soon be raining. I grew angry with myself for not taking the mere seconds to note my car's location. Not knowing where my car was parked—in a lot of more than 12,000 spaces—created a significant amount of anxiety.

I don't know how many silver/gray cars there are in the State of Florida, but I'm pretty sure all of them were at Magic Kingdom's parking lot on this particular day. After walking up and down several rows, I felt the first sprinkles of the coming afternoon downpour. I took my best guess as to the vicinity where I thought my car might be and set off into the long rows of vehicles. As many Guests do in a similar situation, I pushed the alarm button on my car key with the hope my car would eventually call out to me.

After twenty sweat-laden minutes, I eventually found my silver car amidst all of the others. The frustration and annoyance, however, took a while to simmer down within me. I guess you could say the moral of the story is to always pay attention, at least when you park, at Walt Disney World.

The truth is, many of us get lost along the way. It isn't just theme park parking lots which cause us to walk in circles. There are numerous reasons, moments, and phases in life when we lose track of specific markers. It can feel as if we are pacing back and forth as we seek any indication of direction. This is human and common to all who dare to journey through their quests.

Part of my goal in writing this book is to not only lay out a simple framework for you to learn how to hear God clearly—but also to figure out how this plays out in a variety of real scenarios in your everyday life. Quests are not only "mountain-top" callings. They can be simple, small, daily—and just as powerful!

We just have to learn how to recognize and respond to them.

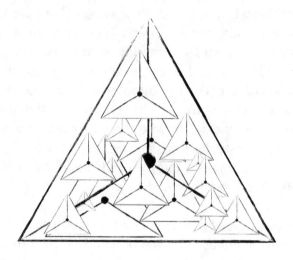

The truth is, it is hard to always know where we are and what is really happening when so much is going on around us. The big adventure we are designed to live throughout our entire lives are filled with smaller quests. Lots of them. These individual calls can last for minutes, months, or even years. God doesn't call us to big things alone—He is faithful to teach us His voice through a handful of simple, daily quests which reveal to us His nature, His timing, and His heart.

However big or small, we wrestle through the reality that Doubt, Fear, and Regret are ready to pounce on each and every quest. It's easy to see how we stall, steer off course, or stop altogether. I think this is why God most often works in us and through us, in the small. As we learn how to overcome Doubt, Fear, and Regret in the smaller quests—we gain confidence in His leading as He teaches us how to navigate through greater calls and challenges.

My desire in this final section is to share how you can be attentive to God's leading in a variety of areas within your own daily life.

How can you keep your focus on God's call at all times?

Let me save you some time: *You can't.*

We are all human. We may get distracted for numerous reasons. Often, we lose our sense of spiritual direction and end up more confused than ever. I don't say this to be discouraging, but rather to be upfront about the challenges we all work through as our human nature distracts from God's call. The good news is, the more we follow God through daily quests, the more we'll have an opportunity to sharpen our hearing and stay in-tune with His leading.

I'm going to share how to use The Quest Compass to maintain clarity, courage, and confidence as God leads you through each and every quest. You'll discover how to know exactly where you are on your quests, what opportunities (and challenges) lay immediately ahead of you and the next steps you'll need to take.

Quests are not only "mountain top" callings. They can be simple, small, daily—and just as powerful. **BIG IDEA**

If you faithfully practice The Quest Compass, you'll discover how intricately invested God is in your life; not just the big stuff, but all the stuff. Even insignificant moments will take on new dimensions of purpose.

You'll be able to quickly diagnose where and why anxiety is creeping into your thoughts. You'll know how to respond quickly to resolve the issue(s). Peace will become a dominant force in your daily life, creating less-and-less room for Doubt, Fear, and Regret to take up permanent residence in your mind.

By also using The Quest Compass in your sphere of influence, you'll be living out Jesus' Great Commission to make disciples in a way which is natural, unforced—and best of all—fruitful.

Now that you have acquired a basic understanding of The Quest Compass, it's time to begin applying it in your own unique circumstances.

This section may feel as if you've just boarded a rollercoaster that is slowly clicking and clattering to the peak of the first drop. We have reached the moment of suspension just before the vehicle tilts downward. It's okay if you want to hold your breath and enjoy the view for a moment. It's also okay if you want to just close your eyes and say a little prayer.

Either way, *here we go.*

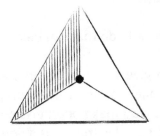

CHAPTER 26:
The Dashboard

"If God gives such attention to the appearance of wild-flowers—most of which are never even seen—don't you think He'll attend to you, take pride in you, do His best for you? What I'm trying to do here is to get you to relax, to not be so preoccupied with getting, so you can respond to God's giving. People who don't know God and the way He works fuss over these things, but you know both God and how He works. Steep your life in God-reality, God-initiative, God-provisions. Don't worry about missing out. You'll find all your everyday human concerns will be met."

- (Jesus) Matthew 6:30-33 MSG

Honest moment: there are things about writing a book which make you question how to communicate in the simplest, most readily accessible way for others to understand a concept. The truth is, I'm deeply passionate about you having the opportunity to hear

215

God clearly, follow Him courageously, and light your world confidently.

But explaining how to do that can be tricky.

I don't want to give the impression you have to work hard to hear one specific, all-encompassing call of God. It isn't as if you make one decision and then your entire life is one big adventure—as if you were living the extended version of *Lord of the Rings*.

On the other hand, I don't want to create anxiety within your life—making you wonder if you could miss God every few minutes because He has so many *micro-missions* for you.

If we aren't careful, our minds can begin to feel like pinball machines with thoughts bouncing around like silver balls triggering all kinds of bells and buzzers. No one can sustain this kind of thinking for long. Eventually, we simply pull the plug and shut down.

This is not how God designed you to live.

His leading is gentle and careful. He promises to sustain you in the longer quests and be with you, coaxing you through the challenges of even the smallest quests. He isn't standing back, as if He were waiting to see if you are going to fail. No. In each and every Quest, He promises to lead and guide you. You'll become more like Him because of it.

What is helpful, however, is a frame of reference for you to have as you move forward. This is why I designed *The Quest Dashboard*. It helps you and me to have three lenses in which to view what God is up to in the three dimensions of our lives which really matter:

1. Our relationship with God; **UP:Quest**

2. Our relationships with those who journey with us (Christ-centered community); **IN:Quest**

3. Our relationship with those to whom God has called us to be light; **OUT:Quest**

We will cover each one of these dimensions in the coming final chapters of this book. For now, let's return to the idea that God is always with us, in every quest—big or small—and we have nothing to Doubt, Fear, or Regret. We simply let Him lead us.

———————

My sister, Robin, and I grew up in a healthy, loving home. As kids, we never worried about the stuff of life such as putting a roof over our heads or food on the table. Our mom and dad provided for us and protected us. There was always a strong sense of security. We knew they were near and that was all that mattered.

Even during my school years, which do not hold many pleasant memories because of my ADD, my parents helped me find the clarity, courage, and confidence to always press on. I knew they loved me and wanted nothing but the best for me. I trusted their wisdom and guidance because it was deeply rooted in their love for me. No matter how stressful life might have been around me, I was able to keep my balance and move forward. All because Mom and Dad kept me focused on what mattered most.

God calls us to trust Him in the same childlike way.

Trust isn't a blind faith but a *childlike faith*. A faith which knows from experience that God has never failed. He can be trusted no matter what—even if we don't fully understand what He's up to. If we keep our eyes on Him, we can maintain our balance and keep moving forward.

 BIG IDEA This kind of trust is not a blind faith but a childlike faith. A faith which knows from experience that God has never failed.

I don't think anyone could put it better than the Apostle Paul, when he wrote in his letter to the Philippians:

I'm not saying that I have this all together, that I have it made. But I am well on my way, reaching out for Christ, who has so wondrously reached out for me. Friends, don't get me wrong: By no means do I count myself an expert in all of this, but I've got my eye on the goal, where God is beckoning us onward—to Jesus. I'm off and running, and I'm not turning back.

- Philippians 3:12-14 MSG

Paul, the author of the majority of the New Testament, understood the need to stay focused on what mattered most. He knew how overwhelming life can be. He, of all people, could speak from experience when it came to difficulty.

He clearly understood how Doubt, Fear, and Regret always lurked to draw him off course. That's why he constantly reminded us to stay focused.

Jesus fully understood the importance of focus and rhythm. In fact, He lived His everyday life in perfect focus and perfect balance.

We see throughout the Gospels how Jesus actually had three focuses and kept them in rhythm/tune with each other. He modeled for us how to use small, ordinary moments and yet be intentional about our over-arching purpose in life. Jesus consistently lived an UP:Quest with God, an IN:Quest with those in His inner circle, and an OUT:Quest with those in the world around Him.

He understood the importance and connection of all three.

Jesus was the "Quest Master," so to speak. He had the full knowledge of how all three were intertwined, and in essence, how they worked together to form one life-quest—to do the will of God. Jesus lived intentionally aware of His relationship with His Father, with His disciples, and with those beyond.

For you and me, Jesus' approach might look like a dashboard. I consider a dashboard an overview space—a way for us to intentionally mirror the way Jesus tended to His various relationships.

By way of The Quest Dashboard, we are able to monitor three different Quest Compasses, each representing one of the three dimensions of our lives: God, our Christ-centered community, and the everyday world around us.

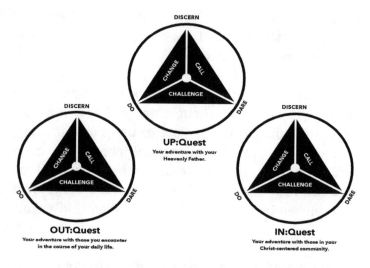

UP:Quest
Your adventure with your
Heavenly Father.

OUT:Quest
Your adventure with those you encounter
in the course of your daily life.

IN:Quest
Your adventure with those in your
Christ-centered community.

We do not have to allow ourselves to become overwhelmed, constantly wondering when we will hear God about an area of our life. He is always leading us. We can know where we are on each compass to determine what we need to *DO* to move forward.

In the context of all three compasses, it is important to note that every one of us is strong in one type of compass. There's one we will always gravitate towards.

For example, because I was a worship leader for many years, my focus favored the UP:Quest. I loved to sit in my office or studio, writing songs which gave me an avenue to express my love for God. I treasured my time alone with Him. But I pursued this to the detriment of my IN:Quest (nurturing relationships in my family and in my church) and my OUT:Quest (intentionally building relationships with those who didn't know God). What I considered to be spiritual solitude became isolation. There were times I didn't seek God's leading in the other two vital areas of my life at all. I only wanted to experience Him in one way, which happened to be the most comfortable way for me.

As I began developing the Quest Compass, I discovered how I actually ignored two other crucially important areas of my life. It was a sobering revelation. It caused me to learn the art of balance in living the adventure God has designed for me.

The Quest Dashboard enables each of us to honestly assess where God is leading us in all areas of life. It reveals what needs to be adjusted and how to make those adjustments.

It helps us to focus and find the balance which Jesus modeled so well in the course of His ministry. We can actually measure our progress as we move forward in all three areas. We can find the joy which comes in seeing God at work in all areas of our lives as He works with each of us to expand His Kingdom Influence.

In the next three chapters, we will look at each quest on the dashboard and learn what it means for you to grow in all three—thereby thriving in your overall adventure.

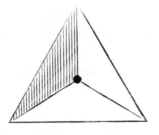

CHAPTER 27:
UP:Quest

YOUR ADVENTURE WITH YOUR HEAVENLY FATHER

"The Son can't independently do a thing, only what He sees the Father doing. What the Father does, the Son does. The Father loves the Son and includes Him in everything He is doing."

- (Jesus) John 5:19, 20 MSG

You and I have been invited into a partnership with God to do amazing things in this world. I don't know about you, but I have a tendency to grow impatient and often run ahead of God. I catch myself trying to do things He hasn't asked me to do. I begin to stumble over myself and become my own worst enemy.

Even though Jesus was the Son of God and had the very nature of God, He knew He could never fulfill His purpose in this world apart from His Heavenly Father. From the very beginning, Jesus, being one with God, never took His eyes off Him. Even when tempted by Satan in the wilderness with promises of earthly Comfort, Credibility, and Control—Jesus responded faithfully by putting God front and center as His focus.

Jesus modeled oneness with His Heavenly Father. We are offered the same.

This is why your UP:Quest Compass focuses on your relationship with God. He wants to transform you into the mirror image of Jesus. To do this, He needs to take you through uncharted adventures which reveal and remove all hindrances in order to replace them with more-and-more of His character.

Jesus wants to lead you through quests which will:

Reveal and remove your indifference and replace it with His love.

Reveal and remove your fleeting happiness and replace it with His joy.

Reveal and remove your conflicts and replace it with His peace.

Reveal and remove your impatience and replace it with His perseverance.

Reveal and remove your secret thoughts of revenge and replace them with His kindness.

Reveal and remove your animosity and replace it with His goodness.

Reveal and remove your hypocrisy and replace it with His faithfulness.

Reveal and remove your hard-heartedness and replace it with His gentleness.

Reveal and remove your over-indulgences and replace them with His self-control.

Your UP:Quest will always be an internal adventure of *revelation, surrender, and discovery.*

UP:Quest

**Your adventure with your
Heavenly Father.**

As you walk with Jesus, He will REVEAL the stuff of life you shouldn't be holding onto. These are the burdens you were never meant to carry, yet you've grown accustomed to their weight.

- Maybe it's anger toward someone that you've held onto for a long time.

- Maybe it's an inability to forgive a hurt which cut you deeply.

- Maybe it is a sin-habit you can never seem to break.

Each of these, along with a pile of other possibilities, are areas within your own INWARD focus. This does not mean you beat yourself up—it simply means you are faithful to always allow God's leading as you let Him mold and shape you from the inside.

It is impossible to list every single burden one can carry in his or her heart. Like everyone else, you have secret places in your heart where those burdens reside. Regardless of what you carry, it's something God wants you to surrender to Him. Most likely it will be quite difficult to release into His hands. You might even try to hide something from Him. That won't work. You'll simply look like a child trying to deny they broke a vase, while holding an incriminating piece in their hand. Hiding your fears, faults, fractures, and failures is pointless because He knows everything about you. *Ev-er-y-thing.* Remember: He loves you—even when you try to hide things from Him.

Because of the intimate knowledge He has of you, He yearns to bring you into freedom and peace which only He can provide. You won't find it anywhere else or with anyone else. He invites you to be completely open and brutally honest with Him. He already knows. He simply wants you to acknowledge what you are wrestling with.

With great wisdom, the writer of one of the Psalms shared how he did not want to hide anything from God. He even invited God to reveal it:

Investigate my life, O God, find out everything about me; Cross-examine and test me, get a clear picture of what I'm about; See for Yourself whether I've done anything wrong—then guide me on the road to eternal life.

- Psalm 139:23, 24 MSG

Once God has *REVEALED* it, He wants to *REMOVE* it from you and set you free of its weight. This doesn't mean it leaves easily. The challenge comes in actually surrendering what God wants to remove. He won't yank it out of your hands; you must give it to Him willingly. It may need to be repeatedly given over until you are completely free of it. It's worth it, because Jesus points out how it's infinitely better to surrender what you're holding onto than to continue stumbling beneath its increasingly crushing weight.

"Anyone who intends to come with Me has to let Me lead. You're not in the driver's seat; I am. Don't run from suffering; embrace it. Follow Me and I'll show you how. Self-help is no help at all. Self-sacrifice is the way, My way, to saving yourself, your true self. What good would it do to get everything you want and lose you, the real you? What could you ever trade your soul for?"

- (Jesus) Mark 8:34-37 MSG

Once you have released whatever God has revealed to you, He won't leave you exposed and vulnerable. He

REPLACES what you have surrendered with something much easier to carry. It's always a little piece of Himself—something only He can provide.

Maybe it's an unexplainable internal peace, even though you are in the midst of a conflict.

Maybe it's an indescribable joy, even though you are walking through a season of sorrow.

Maybe it's simply patience with someone who everyone else has grown frustrated with.

Whatever He gives you in exchange for what you've surrendered, it will be wonderful compared to what you knew before letting go. Jesus said it this way:

"...I won't lay anything heavy or ill-fitting on you. Keep company with Me and you'll learn to live freely and lightly."

- (Jesus) Matthew 11:30 MSG

God will take you on adventures which will definitely change the world through you. But first, He must change what is going on within you. It does not happen all at once. It's a life-long adventure filled with one quest—*a call, a challenge, and a change*—after another. Each one offers you the opportunity to draw closer and closer to God as you let go of more-and-more of your own Comfort, Credibility, and Control.

Be willing to take time to examine your heart, because that's where God is working. Whether you are reading the Bible, spending time in prayer, having a conversation with the person who is mentoring you, or anything else which causes you to be aware that God is up to something—these are significant moments.

Is God REVEALING something?

Whether it is a sin, temptation, hurt, or affliction—take time to acknowledge it. Don't make excuses. At the same time, be completely honest as to how you ended up with it.

Is God REMOVING something?

Do what you must to surrender it. Do you need to turn away from something which is damaging your relationship with God? Do you need to forgive someone, or to let go of a prejudice you carry towards another? It's time to allow God to have it once and for all.

Is God REPLACING something?

Accept it with joy and explore it. Whatever God is offering to you is an incredible gift. He wants you to embrace it and enjoy it.

When God replaces something we've released, it's like moving from grayscale to technicolor. It's Christmas morning and you get to open the most amazing present under the tree. Just remember as you enjoy it, to take the time to thank Him for it. It makes Him smile over you more than you'll ever know.

The quest of *Reveal-Release-Replace* is the hardest of all. However, it's worth the journey, even with its emotional bumps and bruises.

There's a saying traditionally attributed to Michelangelo which says, "Every block of stone has a statue inside it and it is the task of the sculptor to discover it." With each UP:Quest, God is sculpting you. He knows exactly what the sculpture looks like. He knows what's in the stone and chips away at what isn't of Him. This will continue until one day when the work of art will be liberated from its hard-stone fortress.

 BIG IDEA Your UP:Quest will always be an internal adventure of revelation, surrender, and discovery.

A quest, whether big or small, is the tool in God's hands which releases the priceless work of art He originally designed you to be.

Over the course of time, you'll notice your default reactions and responses will come from a motive of love and not of self-preservation. You'll begin to think like Jesus, talk like Jesus, and act like Jesus. Your UP:Quest will become a moment-by-moment adventure, always leading you to the most fulfilling relationship of all: your loving Creator.

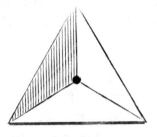

CHAPTER 28:
IN:Quest

YOUR ADVENTURE WITH THOSE
ON THE JOURNEY WITH YOU

**"Who do you think are My mother and brothers?"
Looking around, taking in everyone seated around Him,
He said, "Right here, right in front of you—My mother
and My brothers. Obedience is thicker than blood. The
person who obeys God's will is My brother and sister
and mother."**

- (Jesus) Mark 3:33-35 MSG

Jesus was always intently aware of what His Heavenly
Father was doing. He also remained mindful of all which
was happening among those who followed Him. To Him,
they were family. Even though thousands came to see
Him and listen to Him, the Bible tells us there were 72 to
120 followers whom Jesus considered to be in His circle.

Jesus was closer to some of them than others. The twelve
disciples certainly were with Him every day throughout

the course of His 3+ years of ministry. Among the twelve, Jesus paid special attention to Peter, James, and John. Out of those three, Peter seemed to be treated as a best friend.

Jesus made no differentiation between His blood family from those who were His followers. He prioritized His investment in those who placed their trust in Him as if they were blood family—because as far as He was concerned, they were.

As God in the flesh, Jesus could have done His ministry alone, but He chose not to. He wanted to model for us how our quests should not be pursued alone.

We need the encouragement and challenge of those who journey with us. At the same time, we also need to be encouragers and challengers to our fellow journeyers. As we grow keenly aware of God's activity inside us (UP:Quest), we should also become increasingly aware of His activity among us within the relationships closest to us (IN:Quest).

Throughout the Gospels, Jesus gave extremely clear instructions how His Church should function. It was at His last meal with His disciples and those closest to Him, where He summed up all He had taught in one simple, yet profound statement:

"Let Me give you a new command: Love one another. In the same way I loved you, you love one another. This is how everyone will recognize that you are My disciples —when they see the love you have for each other."

- John 13:34-35 MSG

There are three dynamics at play in this new command Jesus gave to His disciples:

1. "Love one another."
2. "In the same way I loved you…"
3. "This is how everyone will recognize that you are My disciples…"

IN:Quest

Your adventure with those in your Christ-centered community.

"LOVE ONE ANOTHER"

94 times in the New Testament you'll read verses which include the words, "one another." Every time they are used they speak of love (John 15:12), unity, (Mark 9:50, John 6:43) or humility (John 13:14, Galatians 5:13). This makes sense because they are the defining marks of what family should be. Who wouldn't want to be part of a group which was truly loving, unified, and humble toward one another?

This is how the Church is supposed to be: a family *void* of manipulation, gossip, positioning, guilt-tripping, or backstabbing. There's enough of that in the world around us. You see it at work, school, the gym, the store, and anywhere else you find people. As followers of Jesus, we are called to be above this kind of behavior. Unfortunately, that's not always the case. But lest you think I'm throwing stones, I'll be the first to confess I've been guilty of all of the above at one time or another. *How about you?*

You'd think trying to get a handle on "love one another" would be enough for us. Jesus could've stopped right there. For us to truly love one another is a tall order in and of itself. Yet, in the same command, He makes a clarification and raises the stakes even higher. His words become like a laser pointer, zeroing in on what it will take to see this kind of love saturate His family.

"IN THE SAME WAY I LOVED YOU..."

Jesus demonstrated His love by giving His life—literally. The love He had for us was sacrificial from beginning to end.

Think of yourselves the way Christ Jesus thought of Himself. He had equal status with God but didn't think so much of Himself that He had to cling to the advantages of that status no matter what. Not at all. When the time came, He set aside the privileges of deity and took on the status of a slave, became human!

Having become human, He stayed human. It was an incredibly humbling process. He didn't claim special privileges. Instead, He lived a selfless, obedient life and

then died a selfless, obedient death—and the worst kind of death at that—a crucifixion.

- Philippians 2:5-8 MSG

Jesus positioned Himself as a bondservant. A bondservant is someone who serves others without any form of compensation. Even though He was God in the flesh, He placed others' needs above His own. He spent His ministry *lifting* others up. Whether He was teaching, healing, encouraging, or forgiving—He was committed to moving others closer to God, even at His own expense.

As God in the flesh, Jesus could have done His ministry alone, but He chose not to.

BIG IDEA

Today, He challenges us to constantly *lift* each other up; to pour out our lives for the sake of our brothers and sisters—considering them to be more important than ourselves. Even when we don't want to.

The Apostle Paul understood the overwhelming challenge this kind of love presents.

Live creatively, friends. If someone falls into sin, forgivingly restore him, saving your critical comments for yourself. You might be needing forgiveness before the day's out. Stoop down and reach out to those who are oppressed. Share their burdens, and so complete Christ's law. If you think you are too good for that, you are badly deceived.

- Galatians 6:1-3 MSG

Looking to Christ as our example, we soon discover that putting anyone who is a member of His family—our family—ahead of our own Comfort, Credibility, and Control is the way of Jesus. Regardless of how He calls you and me to serve His family, it can often be messy, inconvenient, and filled with disappointment. That's a family. We love each other no matter what, and it's the challenge He invites us to joyfully face.

But it's not all just thistles and thorns. The relational challenges which lay before us will also reveal break-throughs, miracles, fruitfulness, and more joy and peace than we could ever have any other way.

But Jesus isn't through. It's as if He's saying, "But there's more!" He finishes this new commandment with a beautiful promise:

"THIS IS HOW EVERYONE WILL RECOGNIZE THAT YOU ARE MY DISCIPLES..."

By loving each other in a way which surpasses any form of temporary love the world can offer, we (Jesus' family) are able to demonstrate what true love really looks like. It becomes a light to those around us, illuminating the truth of who God is and what He promises to do for those who surrender their lives to Him.

The IN:Quest has no loopholes. It's about loving each other without condition, lifting up each other without condition, and being a light for others to see without condition. After all, this is how Jesus loves us.

Being human, this depth of love is beyond comprehension. Let's admit it; family members can often let us down. That's the reality of life. But, we shouldn't turn our backs on them. Remember, the disciples abandoned Jesus at the moment of His greatest need for family. But He never abandoned them. They had let Him down, yet He never gave up on them.

The unconditional love He spoke of at His last supper was on full display in the early days of the Church:

And all the believers lived in a wonderful harmony, holding everything in common. They sold whatever they owned and pooled their resources so that each person's need was met. They followed a daily discipline of worship in the Temple followed by meals at home, every meal a celebration, exuberant and joyful, as they praised God. People in general liked what they saw. Every day their number grew as God added those who were saved.

- Acts 2:44-47 MSG

The last couple of verses are incredibly powerful. The people outside the Church were watching what was happening inside the Church. They liked what they saw. We know this because the very next verse tells us they wanted to know this Jesus and be a part of His family.

Not to make light of Jesus' commandment, but if you think about it, this commandment is the best form of promotion a church could ever have. It's one thing to have a tag line which says, "Loving God and loving people" on a billboard, a bumper sticker that states, "Believe, Belong, Become." or a T-shirt which reads, "Encounter More."

It's another thing for the world to see it actually lived out, up close and personal.

How you love others in Jesus' family proves Jesus is real, that you know Him personally, and that others are welcome to be a part of it.

It seems to me like Jesus had it right all along.

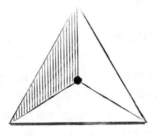

CHAPTER 29:
OUT:Quest

YOUR ADVENTURE IN THE WORLD AROUND YOU

"God authorized and commanded Me to commission you: Go out and train everyone you meet, far and near, in this way of life, marking them by baptism in the threefold name: Father, Son, and Holy Spirit. Then instruct them in the practice of all I have commanded you. I'll be with you as you do this, day after day after day, right up to the end of the age."

- (Jesus) Matthew 28:18-20 MSG

If you've seen the Disney-Pixar film, "UP," you are familiar with the declaration, "Adventure is out there!"

Rather than giving away the plot, I'll just tell you the over-arching theme is how adventure is not something which can be experienced from the comfort of our living rooms or explored from the safety of our sofas. And—let me add—adventure can't thrive inside the four walls of our church buildings.

Adventure is *out there.*

When Jesus gave His disciples His final instructions here on earth, He made it very clear they were to carry on the adventure He had begun three years earlier. He told them He had all authority to send them out as His emissaries to advance all they had learned while He had been with them. They were commissioned to go to the ends of the earth. He even told them He would be with them wherever they went.

I'm sure they had a few questions forming in their minds. I know I would've had a few.

But there was Jesus, raised from the dead, standing before His disciples, telling them He was placing His mission into their hands to steward and carry on.

The mission was simple: Make disciples.

Jesus had modeled this for them for more than three years. They had been with Jesus almost the entire time. Now, it was their turn to do for others what He had done for them. They knew exactly what He was calling them to do.

It's the same mission He is calling you and me to carry out.

Over the course of my time in ministry, I've come to the surprising and sad realization that few followers of Jesus are actually living out this calling entrusted to them, even though it is truly a command of Christ. The hard reality is this: to be mature disciples of Jesus, we must be making disciples.

When you think about it, it's in our spiritual DNA.

Maturing zebras reproduce zebras.
Maturing elephants reproduce elephants.
Maturing birds reproduce birds.
Maturing apple trees reproduce apple trees.
Maturing disciples reproduce...well, you understand where I'm going with this.

Jesus calls you to be His disciple. This includes being a Disciplemaker.

To be mature disciples of Jesus, we must be making disciples. **BIG IDEA**

So, what does "being a Disciplemaker" look like?

A COMMISSION

A disciple of Jesus is someone who has placed their life into His hands, because of who He is (the Son of God), what He has done (He gave His life for their redemption), and they have committed to grow in Jesus' character and competencies. They embrace His identity *AND* His calling; His obedience, *AND* His mission.

At this point you might be saying, "His mission? I don't know how to do that."

My response is an encouraging smile and a simple, "Yes, you do."

I am absolutely certain that even if you decided to follow Jesus yesterday, you could begin to make a disciple today. You already have one day of experience over someone who is yet to make the decision you made yesterday. You know stuff. You've seen stuff. You already have something to share. You have been on a journey to know God. Now, you simply have to share it.

Jesus doesn't ask you to be a perfect example, just a *living* example.

So how do you start? *Where do you start?*

OUT:Quest

Your adventure with those you encounter in the course of your daily life.

A CONNECTION

God wants you to start making disciples first with those who are around you. This includes those whom you are already connected to—the people with whom you have the most in common. It's the friends in your life who see up close how God is working in you (if you are being transparent about your journey).

These people likely aren't followers of Jesus yet.

No problem. Disciplemaking begins before conversion. Jesus called His disciples before most of them truly believed who He was. They followed because they were curious. You'll have others around you who are like that too. Building connections is all about bridges.

You'll need time to understand someone's needs, dreams, hopes, and fears. Then, with prayer, you're able to *DISCERN* how God wants you to disciple them—to lead them to a place where they can explore Jesus.

A quest, or numerous quests, are often part of this process. This is where the *DISCERN*, *DARE*, and *DO* of The Quest Compass come into play. You need to listen for God's leading and then act in accordance with His call.

Disciplemaking is not rocket science. Jesus wouldn't commission you to make disciples and then make it so complicated that few would ever attempt it. That's simply not who Jesus is or how He works. This doesn't mean the call is easy. It's incredibly challenging and you'll need the Holy Spirit to give you the strength, patience, and wisdom to do it.

But herein lies the adventure. God will do things you need Him to do in ways which will surprise, even amaze you. You'll soon discover you are in partnership with God as both of you work together to expand His Kingdom. You'll make mistakes. You'll say and do things you'll wish you could take back. That's okay.

The disciples made a lot of mistakes as they grew into the call Jesus had issued to them.

The point is, they kept going! The Holy Spirit took care of the rest.

By bridging Jesus' commission to make disciples of the people you already connect with, you'll be well on your way to seeing God's power at work around you, as He makes His presence known time and time again.

A COMMUNITY

Whether you have one, two, four, or even eight people you are investing in—you'll become aware that you have a community.

Community is a word which comes from "common unity." This is also where we get the word, "communion." There is something beautiful about God at the center of a community.

Your dinner table becomes a sacred space.
Your living room transforms into a holy place.
Even a table at Starbucks can be a space where
heaven intersects with earth.

The beautiful part is you don't have to force it. Your life becomes a hub for those who are learning from you. Their journey ebbs and flows with the predictable patterns you establish with them individually and/or together.

"And when two or three of you are together because of Me, you can be sure that I'll be there."

- (Jesus) Matthew 18:20 MSG

To be clear, Jesus isn't saying He won't be around when you're alone. He's saying you'll experience something of Him which is more tangible when you gather with others who have the same heart for Him as you do.

Kingdom community simply happens when we give people within our everyday world access to our lives so they can see Jesus. Then, based upon how God is working in them, we have the opportunity to invite them into the same adventure we are living.

That's the sweet fruit produced from your OUT:Quest.

When you live your life as a mission for Jesus, every quest you step into will have eternal consequences. Every word you speak on behalf of Jesus and every action you take for the sake of His Kingdom will make a difference beyond anything you could ever envision.

Jesus started His ministry by inviting others to follow Him. He wrapped up His ministry on earth by sending the same people into the world to make disciples and live the adventure of Kingdom Influence. Jesus has invited you to follow Him. Now He sends you into the world to do the same.

Make no mistake.

Adventure is out there!

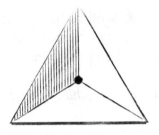

CHAPTER 30:
The Most Important
Chapter in this Book

There is one word you have never read throughout the course of this book. I've deliberately left it out. It is a word which is often used in conjunction with the subject "of faith." You won't find it here. And I have good reason to exclude it from everything you have read in the last 29 chapters.

The word is *RISK*.

As I have shared The Quest Compass with others, the common response centers around the risk involved in walking by faith. To tell you the truth, I still catch myself weighing the risks against the actions of my faith. The framework of The Quest Compass has helped me to question less than I used to, but that doesn't mean I am immune to the influence of Doubt, Fear, and Regret. Sometimes they still get the best of me. They will get you too. It's okay. God offers every morning as a do-over.

So why did I avoid using the word "risk?"

Just before I began writing this book, God revealed something to my heart which has deepened my understanding of trust and obedience:

You risk nothing if everything you have belongs to Jesus!

If you have placed your trust in Jesus Christ, you have surrendered everything to Him:

Your life.
Your family.
Your home.
Your career.
Your reputation.
Your bank account.
Your hopes and dreams.
The list could go on for days.

When we choose to follow Jesus, everything takes a backseat in obedience to Him. I'm not saying He doesn't care about your life, family, home, etc. The opposite is true. He cares for every aspect of your life beyond measure. Because of His love for you, He CALLS you to place Him above everything else. He wants to prove to you He's worth it!

Of course, this is where the CHALLENGE appears.

If you feel you are *risking* something, you must ask yourself if you've truly surrendered it to Jesus.

Ouch.

But let's look at it from a different perspective; a higher perspective: Our God-given quests are less about risk and more about reward. Our attention should never be drawn to what we perceive will be lost, but to what most certainly will be gained.

The life of a Christian holds a call to great sacrifice. But sacrifice does not win us God's favor (we already have it). Rather, we are called to enjoy—through utter dependence—the provision, protection, power, and promises of our Creator. It is how we were designed to live.

This is what makes life interesting. This is where the adventure happens. This is how God works to change the world around us.

But adventure doesn't result only from the surrender of the big things in life. It also happens in the little things. It's a decision to answer God's call in the seemingly insignificant, inconvenient moments. Though they may not seem of great significance at the time, these quests are equally important. You can be assured each and every one of them matters to God. It's our obedience in the great and small quests which unleash the adventure you and I dream of experiencing.

This is why The Quest Compass is beneficial, helping you and me to hear God clearly, follow Jesus courageously, and light our world confidently.

We can actually have the kind of life the Bible describes when it says:

God can do anything, you know—far more than you could ever imagine or guess or request in your wildest dreams! He does it not by pushing us around but by working within us, His Spirit deeply and gently within us.

- Ephesians 3:20 MSG

Your true quest—above all others—is to be the unique reflection of God you were created to be. You don't have to compare yourself to anyone else. All you have to do is listen to God, follow Jesus, and be a light to the world. I pray fervently that The Quest Compass will lead you faithfully into such adventure.

In the introduction of this book, I addressed four types of people. Allow me to close out this book by addressing those same four groups:

If you are new to Jesus and are excited about what lies ahead: Don't let anyone or anything steal your joy of living for Jesus. Learn to recognize His voice and be ready to act when He tells you to. Expect the unexpected. Be ready to share your story. Be on the lookout for those whom God will lead you to pour your life into. Keep moving forward.

If you are curious and simply trying to figure out who Jesus is: Keep your heart and mind open to His presence. If you seek Him, you will find Him. He is closer to you than your own heartbeat. Invite Him to reveal Himself to you. And be ready when He does, because now you know the adventure that awaits you!

If you have followed Jesus for some time but have become stuck: I pray this book has given you the inspiration to move beyond the borders of a comfortable faith. There are others out there who need to be caught up in your adventure and see God working in your life up close and personal. You have all you need to experience breakthrough after breakthrough for His glory!

If you have been looking for a way to help others to experience the love, truth, mercy, and grace of Jesus: I pray that you apply The Quest Compass daily. The more you do, you will recognize when God is up to something. You will see how He desires to work in you and through you, with anyone, anywhere, anytime. May you be fruitful and multiply the Kingdom Influence He has entrusted you with!

> Your true quest—above all others—is to be the unique reflection of God you were created to be. You don't have to compare yourself to anyone else.

I pray all of us—each in our own unique way—will shine brightly as the reflections of God we are created to be. Together, I pray we blanket this broken world with the glory of Jesus from this day until He returns!

Glory to God in the church! Glory to God in the Messiah, in Jesus! Glory down all the generations! Glory through all millennia! Oh, yes!
                                        - Ephesians 3:21 MSG

The best is yet to come!

ACKNOWLEDGEMENTS

Cassandra Smith and Aletheia Press: You pursued me with the idea of a book for two years before I relented. You helped me shape this project into what everyone now holds in their hands. God bless you for your perseverance.

Jim Thacker: You are a true friend, encourager, and a master wordsmith.

Rod Pasch: Thank you for accompanying me on the twists and turns of this wild ride.

Aaron and Michelle Cantrell: Thank you for being with me from the time this was just a crazy idea. No turning back now.

Marisol Barr and Justin Sayles: Thank you for being my first readers and constructive critics.

Glen Schrieber and my fellow EFCA Southeast District Pastors: Thanks for encouraging me to play in my sandbox. I hope this book proves it was worth it.

Those who hosted and/or participated in my Quest Workshops: Thank you for affording me the opportunity to share this content in its infant stages.

Cast Member Church Leadership Team (Ed Kaylor, Greg Cole, Rod Pasch): Thank you for challenging me to not conform and stay out on the fringe.

Cast Member Church Communi-Ds: You are the fruit of God's vision for Disney and I love you all dearly.

Mike Breen: "Hero" is a dangerous word to apply to someone, but you've earned it. Few have influenced me as you have. Thank you for being someone worthy of imitation.

Lucia, Marisol, and Miguel: With all my heart, I thank you for your patience, kindness, love, and support throughout this crazy, creative process. I can't imagine having embraced this adventure without you. I love you.

Jesus: This is for you and your Kingdom. To You alone be the glory.

...AND THE ADVENTURE CONTINUES!

you would like to experience more of The Quest Compass, you can participate in a one-day Quest workshop at Walt Disney World (the home of Cast Member Church) or host a workshop at your own location. Either way, you'll have the opportunity to be inspired by Steven Barr and learn to process and personalize The Quest Compass in your own context.

If you would like to go even deeper, you can join one of Steven's online Quest Groups and learn how to mentor others using The Quest Compass as a discipling tool.

Visit DisciplemakingSolutions.com to learn more.

DisciplemakingSolutions.com